THE ENCOUNTER

ABIDING WITH GOD FOR 40 DAYS

JACK E. DITT JR.

Cover Artwork by Janice Vancronkhite
Edited by Christopher DeGueurce

Notes:
Some of the names herein have been changed to protect the privacy of individuals.

Unless otherwise noted, all Scriptures have been taken from the New King James Version Bible.

DEDICATION

I dedicate this work to my wife and treasure for life, Stacey, to our four daughters, Cassie, Olivia, Sarah, and Hannah, and our grandchildren. To them and the reader I pray that you are awakened and touched by my most sincere effort to reach you...that you all shall run faster and farther in the Lord than the mind can even begin to comprehend, becoming all that which "the creation is groaning and travailing for," on Earth as it is in Heaven.

ACKNOWLEDGEMENTS

It is a pleasure to recognize my friends, all of whom I also refer to as family, who contributed to THE ENCOUNTER. COL Tom Hesterman, my brother David, Mickey Chance, Mike Conkle, and Stephen Alls all helped me with editing of both content and grammatical issues. My colleague, Bill McCollum helped greatly with editing during the initial stages of this endeavor.

A great deal of this story has to do with my mentors or spiritual mother and fathers. There is no ENCOUNTER without the late Jack McClendon and his wife, Pat McClendon who, thankfully, just moved back to Shreveport. My current mentor, spiritual father, pastor, life coach, and close friend, Brad McClendon, who is also moving to Shreveport, I am forever indebted to, for his most loving mentorship and fathering of Stacey, my kids, and myself. Over the last ten years Brad has visited us multiple times annually, usually staying from Tuesday or Wednesday until Monday. We recently estimated that he has spent more than a year in our home with us. We also recently kidded that we could make a most interesting movie out of all of the life moments we have shared. It is this recklessly abundant life which Brad has coached us to live, following himself and more importantly, Jesus. I'm quite certain that His life was radical beyond comprehension and especially any comparison.

An unquantifiable appreciation is owed to my mother and late father, Helen and Jack E. Ditt, for teaching us a fear of the Lord during our upbringing, which carried over to college life and thereafter. Until I was forty, I knew who my Savior was with the conviction of every sin that I committed, from my upbringing; I just didn't embrace Him as Lord until later. My wife Stacey should author a book about her life. She has been my true love for more than 25 years. She is the spiritual one who has put up with me while also making life so amazingly wonderful. She has always loved me with ALL of her life, something I aspire to do someday, hopefully soon.

Although I've known him less than a year, Westley Roderick has quickly become a friend and talent who has helped me with the cover design, formatting, and general advice with this venture.

Finally, this work would have never come to fruition without a chance encounter with Chris DeGueurce whom I direct a tremendous amount of gratitude towards for his skill, diligence, and sense of humor in completing the editorial work involved. One night, Stacey and I were dining at a local downtown restaurant/pub when the Lord spoke to me that the man behind the bar was my editor. I knew that he was smart, but recently I asked him if he ever took the SAT exam, to which he replied affirmatively, and that he got a perfect 800 on the verbal portion. He was also a National Merit Finalist in high school. That confirmed to me that I had heard correctly. He has especially inspired me to make myself vulnerable in attempting to reach the heart of the reader. I sincerely hope that indeed I have.

FORWARD

When man has a true encounter with God, no one can take away what he believes about God. For a man with experiential knowledge trumps those who have gathered knowledge. Their experience itself becomes a part of the person's DNA. If they speak of their encounter, it releases that experience in the atmosphere, allowing others to encounter God themselves. Moses was a great example of one who experienced the power of God. After his encounter, Moses became a carrier of that power and was able to bring it to Egypt to set people free from an abusive system of the world. There are several others in the Bible that experience God, including the disciples who after walking with God personally, became world changers. Jack Ditt's writings are not to cause the reader to believe in his opinion about God, but to see people personally experience

God for themselves. There are not many I know who are as passionate about God as Jack Ditt. His heart is to see all experience God so they too can be those who not only know Him, but carry God within their personal lives. The "Encounter" is written just for that, for the reader to "Encounter" God.

Bradford Parks McClendon
Living Vine Ministries, Myrtle Beach, SC

ENDORSEMENTS

"As I read these stories and treasured insights from a life laid down, there were several moments where I felt the tangible presence and power of the Holy Spirit rest on me, recalibrating, reinvigorating. I can feel Jack's reverence and respect for Yahweh in every section."

- Jeremy Shuck, Pastor,
Upper Room, Frisco, TX

"I am honored to be one of the early readers of Jack Ditt's first book, *The Encounter.* This is a wonderful true story of the beginning of Jack's transformational walk with Our Lord Jesus and the impact on his life and the lives of those that know and love him. His transformation and impact continues today through this book and all those Jack personally encounters as a child of God."

"Like an arrow piercing its target, Jack Ditt's passion and dedication to the Lord hits the reader's heart throughout The Encounter. The pages are filled with stories that ignite hunger to experience more with God, while the childlike faith and nature challenge readers to repent back to simple devotion. As you read this book, allow it to set your spirit on fire for a fresh encounter of your own!"

"I invite you to go on a journey with Jack as he shares his "Encounters" with Jesus and then walks them out. This will challenge you to seek after relationship rather than religion. It is a simple treatise in hearing and obeying, then enjoying the results. It will awaken your spirit."

- Phil Dowdy, Overseer,
Forerunner Church, Elizabeth City, NC

"Loved this book. When I read it, I was drawn into an experience with the Lord. This is fresh and alive."

- Randy Strombeck,
Koinonia Ministries, Moravian Falls, NC

"The Encounter will keep you mesmerized about the goodness and faithfulness of God.

You will be challenged to go deeper and also connect with those God sends into your life in a deeper way. Jack's story will definitely stir you up to go after God with a new fervor. You will be inspired to become a Word and Spirit Warrior. It has stirred me and I'm glad to have read it."

- **Scott Nary, Founder**
420 FIRE International, Charlotte, NC

"I started reading *The Encounter* one afternoon and was surprised a couple of hours later that I was having trouble putting it down. Although I love meditating in the Word, every few years I read the Book of Acts as an adventure story coming away inspired by the joy and awe the disciples experienced walking with the Lord. Jack's story has had a similar effect. These pages contain an impartation of worship, love and High Adventure and moreover a vision for the life each of us is called to live."

- *John Michael Murphy,*
Denver, CO

"Encounters with God supernaturally should be normal. And all normal encounters with God revolve around hearing His voice, staying connected to His family, and not being afraid to step out of the box and do something extravagant with Him. And sometimes (if not most of the time), that extravagance seems silly or foolish to both you and others. This book reminds us all that our faith is built on daily encounters, not logic and reason. All of us need our faith to increase for the power of God to be made manifest in our daily lives, and that's what this book will help you find; a greater hunger, thirst, and desire for the more God has in store for our lives."

- David Bendett, Senior Pastor,
Rock City Church, Corpus Christi, TX

"Jack Ditt's The Encounter is a catalyst to an experiential relationship with God. Each testimony and story is pregnant with seeds of faith to take us deeper and closer to the living God, it is like Zechariah mentioned in chapter 4 about the internal eternal awakening towards God.

Expect to step into a greater dimension of intimate friendship with God as you read The Encounter.

- Westley N Roderick,
LoveSpeaks Ministries, Shreveport, LA

PART I

"IN THE NAME OF THE LORD JESUS CHRIST WAKE UP," I SHOUTED.

THE MAN IN THE COMA

Scared to death, Mike and I exited the elevator and began to walk down the poorly lit corridor of the eighth floor of the hospital, wondering what was about to take place. Pondering and trying to picture, playing out mentally the scene set before us, we moved forward slowly toward David's room. Imagine yourself as a relatively new believer in God, having grown up in a mainstream liturgical denomination, and now you are about to be used by God for something of paramount importance, for the first time in your life. While anxious, fearful, and excited for this moment, we believed we had a clear revelation from God that He had sent us for this task at hand. As we approached our destination, we saw a woman we presumed to be David's wife, standing outside the room speaking to several pastors. Seeds of doubt entered my thinking as I contemplated my qualifications to pray for her husband, whom I did not know at all, when her formally educated pastors were already available and with her. I then thought about the many unlearned, meek heroes of the faith that I had read about in the Bible, all of whom seemed unqualified for the greatest of exploits that they had been called to conduct. The common denominator, I thought, with all these men and women, was simply their obedience and raw faith in the One behind the endeavor they were engaged in. There was no turning back. We were committed.

Beforehand Mike and I had decided to meet each other after work outside of the hospital. We did and prayed for the Lord to prepare the way for us upon entering the building. Once we had made it to David's wife, who knew neither of us, she asked what we were doing there. We said that we believed God had sent us specifically to pray for her husband. She told us that he was in bad shape and that the doctors had said he would likely pass during the night. Mike asked if it was OK for us to lay hands on David and pray for him, just as the Bible instructs us. (1) While I don't recall her name, she said that it would be fine, provided we wash our hands in the sink within the room. We thanked her, cleansed our hands, placed them on his bare chest, and prayed with an intensity as though our houses were on fire with our families inside.

MEETING MIKE

Mike and I first met each other in 1990, and it was now November of 2002. Initially I really liked him but didn't like spending much time with him because his disposition and kindness made me uncomfortable, given that I hadn't made a commitment to Christ like he had. His conversing about the Lord made me squirm because I really had nothing experientially speaking to exchange or add...but that would change. I recognized the Truth from my upbringing but had not yet embraced

Him. It took roughly another ten years of running from God, being disgusted with my life of living on the edge, partying, and not facing my real problems or personal issues, until June of 2001 when the Lord made Himself known to me.

Fast forward to November 21 of 2002. Mike and I found ourselves in awe, standing at the bottom of the stairwell of a legal office building near downtown Shreveport. What happened next is difficult to describe. We were both simultaneously overwhelmed by the power of God as His Holy Spirit literally, physically came upon us. For what seemed like fully several minutes, Mike and I were unable to speak as we were enveloped by the most incredibly comforting feelings of love. We just stood there shockingly gazing at each other and wondering what was happening. I had no conception of what was occurring, but I would understand more in the days ahead. Radically inspired, Mike looked at me and said that we were supposed to pray for a man on the 8th floor of

Willis Knighton hospital who had fallen into a fuel truck and subsequently into a coma. As he spoke those words, I too immediately KNEW that we had to go.

Having had the encounter that morning, we had faith and a zealous burden for this venture. "Faith comes by hearing, and hearing by the word of God." (2) Well, we were operating on His faith, having both felt like we knew (and heard) that we needed to be there. Now it was merely an issue of obedience and to let God do the rest. While we didn't really notice anything happening while we prayed for David, we felt especially good about his future wellbeing.

About a week later I received a teaching pamphlet from Andrew Wommack Ministries in Colorado regarding "speaking to the mountain", a phrase from the Gospel of Mark about how to pray specifically for problems. According to Andrew's teaching, the mountain is your problem. Jesus said, "Have faith in God. For assuredly, I say to you, whoever says to this mountain, 'Be removed and be cast into the sea,' and does not doubt in his heart, but believes that those things he says will be done, he will have whatever he says. Therefore I say to you, whatever things you ask when you pray, believe that you receive them, and you will have them." (3)

When I read this, I immediately called Mike and told him that we needed to go back to the hospital and speak to David's mountain.

"In the name of the Lord Jesus Christ wake up!", I shouted to him.

"Sit up and look at us! Coma, be thou removed, and be thou cast into the sea!" David immediately sat up and looked toward us, yet he was still blind. He did, however, come out of his coma! Envision this hospital room backdrop, praying for a complete stranger, who has been given a death sentence, to come out of his coma, then most suddenly he sits up and responds to you. Exhilarating! This large man who woke up to our fervent praying and shouting had been asleep for more than five weeks. On a humorous note, I had such a strong sense of a reverential fear of God and His inspired Word that for a lengthy season, until I learned differently, I actually prayed the Scriptures literally, just as they were written. On this day, I prayed in the King James by shouting, "Coma, be thou removed, and be thou cast into the sea."

THE ENCOUNTER, DAY ONE

What happened the first morning at the stairwell before we prayed for David was something that I had never experienced, and intoxicatingly kicked off my supernatural encounter, yet it took a few months to figure out. But what was also occurring at the same time was the most profound experience with the Lord that I had ever known and will never forget, and only in recent years have

I come to more fully understand it. While I have since had a number of very personal experiences with the Lord Jesus, this one lasted forty days, and each day of it was extremely far-reaching, making me so long for the Lord, to find my way back to that place. This writing is about that encounter, and I remember it well, along with my perspective of the purpose of it, and what some of the accompanying wide-ranging revelations meant and mean, both for me and anybody interested in knowing God like their own father. To understand why God revealed Himself through these intense and mystical experiences, it may help to understand who I was before He spoke to me, to see why I needed Him so badly.

BORN AGAIN

Born in Lebanon, Pennsylvania, I lived the first 23 years of my life mostly in the Commonwealth of Virginia. At the time of my birth, my father was a student at the University of Richmond. After graduation he worked all over Virginia. The oldest of three boys, I attended Lexington area schools before finishing high school in Annville, Pennsylvania. Having become a three-time runner-up in PA State High School track and cross-country championships, I moved back to Lexington, to attend The Virginia Military Institute (VMI) on a partial track scholarship. In the presence of my mom, dad, and high school coach at The Naval Academy, in my very first collegiate track meet, I set the VMI 3000-meter indoor record, and my athletic scholarship was fully upgraded. To this day I still hold a half dozen track and field school records there, to include the metric equivalent of a sub-four-minute mile. In 2003, I was inducted into the VMI Sports Hall of Fame and used the occasion to share my faith with the VMI community for the first time in my life.

My family enjoyed a strong spiritual heritage on both sides. Most notable to me were my humble, loving paternal grandparents, Samuel and Genevieve, and my maternal great, great, great,

great, great grandfather Abraham Niebel, a circuit rider and preacher of the Gospel by horseback in Ohio and Pennsylvania during the 1840s until after the civil war. My mother experienced Jesus when I was in the 9th grade. My father soon followed. Before this their marriage was rocky, but afterwards, they were a wonderful Godly influence upon us three boys. This resulted in a very special fear of the Lord in me which greatly helped to solidify what it meant to walk in righteousness, until I went to college. During those years, including high school, my passion and talent for running formed ever greater parts of my identity, leaving little room for Jesus. I became egotistical and even narcissistic, yet I realized more and more that I was only as good as my last race, with even the best ones fading quickly from my sense of accomplishment. My endurance racing ability spoke prophetically of my identity in Christ, my existential race of life with God, and my ability to suffer and persevere through difficult trials. At the time, however, I ran away from the Lord. I ran only for myself.

Commissioned a 2nd Lieutenant in the USAF upon graduation from VMI, I went through navigation and electronic warfare officer schools in California before moving to Shreveport, Louisiana where I now reside. Once my commitment to the armed forces and flying B-52 bombers had been fulfilled I walked unannounced into the Shreveport office of Legg Mason, a regional brokerage firm, looking for work, and was soon hired. I continued my dream in athletics and got fitter than ever before, running a 5k in 13:49 on July 4th, 1990, in Little Rock, Arkansas, placing me among the swiftest 15 or so middle-distance runners in America. It was such a rush to compete at that level again, besting premier runners from Kenya and leading a couple of future Olympians through most of the race. However, on Thursday when I went out for my recovery run, I could not take a step without excruciating pain in my right knee. Due to knee surgery as a freshman at VMI, I now had osteoarthritis and literally could not run one more day. Having reached the near pinnacle of my sport and ceasing cold turkey the next day turned my dream into a nightmare. So still desperately trying to find myself, my true identity in sport, I soon started weight training fanatically after work and was shortly thereafter proselytized a Shreveport rugby player. My rugby experience was necessary to find, meet, and marry the love of my life, Stacey Chesley. We embraced this cultish sport for a couple of years until my knee swelled with every practice. (I realize the notion of playing rugby with an arthritic knee absent the medial meniscus was incredibly stupid!) Yet we didn't really fit in and lived woefully unfulfilled lives. Still, it didn't take long for me to discover competitive road cycling, a low resistance sport that my knees handled well. In the year 2000 as a 39-year-old, I rode in the Olympic trials, finished in the money, and beat future Tour de France winner, Floyd Landis, by eight places. Nevertheless, I vividly recall standing on the Natchez Trace in Jackson, Mississippi afterwards that day, in tears, while every career running and cycling climax flashed before me. Our daughters were growing up and had their own sports and lives. Where had I been, I thought. It was their turn. Stacey was so kind and close to me as we contemplated a new beginning during our drive home.

Upon reflection it seems that Father God was wooing me to him in order to fill a forthcoming void in my heart and very being. Stacey and I soon started attending a local Methodist church, where she and her parents worshipped. I too grew up Methodist in the northeast. During the next few years I experienced what I would call a double life: the life which I lived on Sundays, and the other life for the next six days. This hypocritical life of playing church, which deep inside I really despised, continued for about seven years until I decided to face my fears and yield to my Lord. I was indeed convicted by the Holy Spirit, especially having witnessed the strong conversions and life that my parents now lived, in Christ. I had also reached a place where I decided to face these certitudes and small group anxiety issues, among other fears. While we all have fear that we are called to overcome, there is often shame in the realization of how silly this can be, yet so powerful and debilitating in our lives when we choose to embrace fear over faith, and attempt to live in the power of our own strength.

In March of 2001 I started attending a men's small group Bible study on Wednesday evenings at the Methodist church. By now I had become aware of the Father drawing me to Him as I loved the fellowship and studying God's Word. (4) After about three months, one evening at the end of the study mostly everyone had departed except for three attendees. I was there only because one of the guys, Anthony, needed a ride that I had promised to deliver. The reason the others stayed was because a man named Lee, was terribly distraught for having just lost his job. He wanted prayer. While the three gentlemen prayed for five or ten minutes, I mostly just stood there in agreement with what I had heard. I took Anthony home, ate dinner, and went to bed.

The next morning was Thursday, June 28th of 2001. I remember it well. I got to the office at about 8 o'clock. Waiting for me in my office was Jim, a retired Colonel and pilot client of mine who owned a furniture store. Jim was a longtime friend. He came by the office once a month for coffee, but never before ten. He explained to me that he had just lost a most valued employee the day before and he didn't know what to do. At that moment a powerful, loving presence of the Lord came over me, and I immediately knew that Lee, for whom we had prayed the night before, would be his new employee. For the first time in my life, I had knowingly witnessed for myself an answer to prayer. I was overwhelmed with emotion and despite my best efforts to keep my composure, I lost all control and didn't care in the least. My Maker, God Almighty, had unmistakably revealed Himself to me. Even though Jim was not a believer he recognized that something powerful had happened to me. I was born again and committed to live my life for and with Christ. (5) It is also so amazing to note that Stacey and I prayed with him years later, on his death bed, with our spiritual mentor and watched him experience God's saving grace and eternal life.

THE 112 GROUP

Riding high, so full of life like never before, I immediately felt compelled to facilitate a morning-breakfast Bible study. I thought at length of everyone in the Shreveport area who had a Godly influence upon me, especially all of those whom I considered to be "super-duper" spiritual. After meeting with a few of these men, we decided to begin a 7 a.m. study. A friend named Robert offered his office for meetings on the top floor of the Beck building in downtown Shreveport. Our first meeting was on Tuesday, the 10th of July 2001. About seven of us met in Robert's office and we started with a verse-by-verse study of the apostle Paul's "Book of Romans". After failing to find anyone to volunteer to lead this endeavor, I was nominated to direct and facilitate the study. The group quickly grew to about fifteen men, hungry for God's Word, and I studied numerous books on Romans to help with our understanding. We moved to several different locations, before ultimately settling down in a law office on East Kings Highway about five minutes from downtown. Every walk of life and vocation was invited and participated in our study. We had lawyers, accountants, businessmen, manufacturing workers, etc. We would go until about 8:15 a.m., studying meticulously every word of the Scriptures, before closing in prayer and heading off to work. We ultimately met about 250 times over five years and covered most of the New Testament through Revelation Chapter 6 and a number of the Old Testament books. We tried many different approaches including utilizing studies that worked through books we obtained through a Baptist bookstore. I soon discovered that many potentially controversial Scriptures were left out of the study books. We wanted to know all of God's word and, therefore, went back to our verse-by-verse methodology, and above all, attempting to rely upon the Holy Spirit. (6)

Early on, thankfully, I learned a powerful, foundational truth that was threefold: that Jesus is God; (7) there is no other way to heaven, God, or eternal life for any man but through the Son of Man; (8) and that ALL Scriptures are inspired by God. (9) This latter point means that it is as if all Scriptures have been God-breathed into that wonderful book. I have read the Bible from cover-to-cover at least thirty times, and I have Never found a Scripture that conflicts with another. (If one finds a potential conflict, he must dig deeper.) Atheists and agnostics may argue, for example, that there are four very different conflicting gospels or renderings of "the good news." That is because Matthew, Mark, Luke, and John all spent time with the Lord Jesus, and they each had different experiences and teachings they felt important to scribe, yet again under the power and anointing of God's Holy Spirit. If four siblings were to write about three and a half years that they spent with their father, all four accounts would be very different. Another favorite Scripture that reinforces this truth is, "In the beginning was the Word, and the Word was with God, and the Word was God...and the Word became flesh and dwelt among us." (10) So what is most important here, is that Jesus is who He and His disciples said He was, and the Bible, which is timeless, is God's inspired Word that points and reveals us to Himself. Jesus came to show us the path to His Father, and He (Jesus) is the same, yesterday, today, and forever. (11)

After more than five especially fruitful years I felt led not to go any further with the book of

Revelation, and ultimately to conclude our study because, I think, the Lord had other plans for all of us. (I have since been inspired to spend hundreds of hours of mostly self-study of this book and have begun some work on a Bible study commentary, a continuing work in progress.) During the five years of our study, the 112 Group provided the means to build a house in Guatemala, dig a water well for an Indian tribe in Venezuela, and fund other mission efforts. Our group was graced by worldly people desperately seeking the Truth, and nearly every walk of life, including several pastors. It was ecumenical, cutting across Catholics, many Protestant denominations, and non-denominational believers. I was eternally blessed by the foundation obtained, a starting place for my understanding of God and His ways, but the best part was the connection and interaction with all the different men who attended.

The first time that I recall ever hearing and recognizing the Lord's voice after my born-again experience had to do with the study group. A Scripture illuminated to me and I heard that we were to name the Bible study the 112 Group after Romans 1:12, which reads, ..."that we may be mutually strengthened and encouraged and comforted by each other's faith, both yours and mine."

Soon after this I was listening to a set of Andrew Wommack Ministry teaching tapes on Colossians and Ephesians. If I were asking the Lord for an answer to a question that I had, I would pray my name into prayers that Paul had written to the Colossians and Ephesians. For example, I would pray, "For this reason we also, since the day we heard it, do not cease to pray for you (Jack), and to ask that you may be filled with the knowledge of His will in all wisdom and spiritual understanding; that you (Jack) may walk worthy of the Lord, fully pleasing Him, being fruitful in every good work and increasing in the knowledge of God; strengthened with all might, according to His glorious power, for all patience and long-suffering with joy; giving thanks to the Father who has qualified us to be partakers of the inheritance of the saints in the light." (12)

And again, "Therefore I also, after I heard of your faith in the Lord Jesus (Jack) and your love for all the saints, do not cease to give thanks for you (Jack), making mention of you in my prayers: that the God of our Lord Jesus Christ, the Father of glory, may give to you the spirit of wisdom and revelation in the knowledge of Him, the eyes of your understanding (Jack) being enlightened; that you may know what is the hope of His calling, what are the riches of the glory of His inheritance in the saints, and what is the exceeding greatness of His power toward us who believe, according to the working of His mighty power which He worked in Christ when He raised Him from the dead and seated Him at His right hand in the heavenly places, far above all principality and power and might and dominion, and every name that is named, not only in this age but also in the age which is to come. And He put all things under His feet, and gave Him to be head over all things to the church, which is His body, the fullness of Him who fills all in all." (13)

Though now rather humorous to me, this methodology worked perhaps a dozen times for me to hear or get an answer from the One whom I refer to as Papa regarding whatever I was dealing with. However, after a few months I noticed that my formulaic and robotic approach wasn't bearing fruit like it previously had, so I stopped praying this way and simply talked with Him. For me, when my approach in communicating with God is communal, just like a small child talking to his father, that is when I seem to hear best. Other times, it seems, require time and persistence before hearing from Father, yet the joy that comes with His delayed response is memorable beyond words.

BACK TO THE ENCOUNTER

It was during our study of the book of Acts that something so special occurred to me. I had been taught that one of the most important reasons to read the Bible was to experience the Lord. In Luke 24 the disciples were told to tarry in Jerusalem until they were endued with power from on high, the source of which being the Promise of the Father. Then in Acts 1 they were told they would receive power when the Holy Spirit came upon them. Acts 2 states that suddenly there came a sound from heaven, as a rushing mighty wind, and it filled the whole house where they were sitting...and they were all filled with the Holy Spirit and began to speak with other tongues, as the Spirit gave them utterance.

The 112 Group had just gone through these passages during our study. Then at the bottom of the stairwell, as we were leaving to go to work, Mike and I were visiting when the Holy Spirit came upon us mightily and filled us. This was the

Promise from the Father, getting Him in spirit; we were endued with power from on high. The Greek word for "power" is *"dunimus"* and means "mighty, resurrection power." Paul wrote, "For the kingdom of God is not in word but in power." (14)

I learned that the most effective evangelism is in power, and generally the greatest power comes when you feel so compassionate for whomever has the need. If you want to see someone changed by God's saving grace, heal them or tell them something about who they are in Christ rather than debate them about some theological argument. That is God's power that comes from the Promise of the Father (Holy Spirit). The reason why we should earnestly desire spiritual gifts (15), which manifest God's awesome power, is so that we can walk in this mighty power, restore life which has been stolen by satan, and be a witness of the Lord's resurrection (16).

I didn't really understand what had happened at the time, but the Lord had filled us with His Spirit, that morning, and endued us with power at precisely the perfect time because He next told us we were to go to the hospital to pray for the man (David) in the coma who was about to die.

This baptism that I experienced, and that John the Baptist spoke about, was a life-changing event for me. "He (Jesus) will baptize you with the Holy Spirit and fire;" precisely what happened to Mike and me while standing that day at the bottom of the stairwell. (17) I was forever changed by this, and it was the beginning of an encounter that would last for forty days. But some other things were transpiring that made little sense at the time. I came home that night after praying for David and did not go to bed. I walked around the house all night just pacing and pondering what was going on. I had so much energy in me I didn't need sleep. It felt like I was cocooned within a force field of love, that I would later understand to be God's glory or goodness, His perfect love. When I reflect back on this time it is still like it happened yesterday. I recall that I would go two or three days without any sleep, go straight to work, glowing and walking continuously in God's presence. His Holy Spirit had given me so much life and energy. Nothing bothered me. People would say terrible things to me, and I would genuinely smile to them and love on them. My best estimate is that during these 40 days I averaged less than two hours of sleep. This was all totally supernatural. I also noticed that I did not need to eat. No caloric intake was necessary to find strength that was already there. I had supernatural energy. During that time, I ate simply because I love good food. These days were easily the most unforgettable and fulfilling for me thus far in my life, where I felt as if I alone was God's son, friend, and treasure. This may be difficult to believe, yet I so can't wait for this to happen again, to encounter Jesus, my Creator, and I know that this most passionate interconnection with the God of the universe is for anybody who desperately wants Him.

THE FIRST NIGHT VISION

On the third day of the encounter I went to bed and was lying on my back about to get some rest when, all of the sudden, the Spirit came over me and my body started vibrating with love and profoundly electrifying energy. This was the most comforting feeling I've ever experienced; I did not want it to stop. Revelation was pouring into me for ten or fifteen minutes about the Lord and His kingdom and His inordinate care for me. This incredibly overwhelming experience is difficult to describe. I opened my eyes and the vibrations and feelings immediately stopped, so I quickly closed them, and the uplifting feelings and electric vibrations continued for what seemed like another ten or fifteen minutes; Father was making Himself known to me. I couldn't possibly go back to sleep for the sensations of love and life were so strong, so I got up and walked around the house for a few hours that passed like minutes, soaking in His abiding presence.

When I did finally go back to bed it started again. His warm, oscillating love resonating throughout every cell of my body, and then a night vision, like a dream began, yet I was completely awake. In the vision I saw all kinds of perfectly white boards floating around in the sky, and then they lined up and formed a white wall that surrounded a cemetery. Behind the cemetery was a red dirt road that went by a mango orchard. Inside the cemetery was a statue of a man named Jesus with a small fence around the statue. I did not hear anything but knew in the vision that this place was Venezuela, a place I had never seen. The vibrating continued a little longer before it finally ended. I jumped out of bed and walked around the house with great joy until daybreak, took a shower, and headed to work, not needing or even contemplating the idea of any sleep this night.

The next morning, I couldn't wait to talk to Mike as I was so excited, and I didn't know anyone else with whom I could discuss this. Upon hearing my story Mike told me that he had had some dreams and visions about some places in Venezuela as well, and that we would be going down there soon when the Lord revealed to us all the necessary steps and players. It is interesting to recall that Mike told me (in error) that if I shared any of these things with my wife Stacey that she would be greatly disturbed, as she was not yet a true believer. What a mistake. Over the next month I would secretly discuss these encounters and revelations with Mike while hiding in my back yard. My bizarre behavior led Stacey to believe that I may be on drugs or having an affair. Ultimately, she confronted me, and I told her everything. (Remember, I wasn't even coming to bed most nights as I would just walk around the house all night, play music, and talk to God.) Stacey met with a couple of the local Methodist pastors, from the church where we were attending, to see what they thought. To our surprise they told her that they didn't believe in healing (They referred to it as faith-healing) and that I had taken the Bible way too literally. They also thought I was likely going through some type of mid-life crisis that would probably soon come to an end.

CONCEALING MY EXPERIENCES FROM STACEY

Stacey and I had some very uncomfortable evenings together; nevertheless, she could tell something powerful had radically changed me. Even though I had shared my vision with her I continued to do things in secret. It was what I did covertly without communicating with her that ultimately brought us to the brink. One night she approached me, crying and upset. We sat down in the living room, and I reiterated my love for her and how I had thought I was doing the right thing. I also explained how she really needed to experience this for herself. This was all so new for us. Our whole lives we had attended church, and yet, missed the entire point: that we were meant to have a real, tangible relationship with our Maker who so desperately wants to share and help in our rich, abundant earthly walk. I eventually learned that the longer one stays in a routine of, for example, monotonously plodding to church on Sundays, Wednesday Bible studies, etc., or doing activities or works to earn something from God, the more difficult it becomes to truly recognize and experience the Lord in our daily lives.

It is interesting that as I write this one of our daughters is on her honeymoon. Marriage is a prophetic symbolic lifelong experience that so parallels the relationship we are supposed to have with Jesus. In Scripture we are the bride of Christ and Jesus is the Bridegroom. The church is Mother and obviously called to intimacy with Papa, Father God. Many, if not most, of our doctrines, traditions and rituals that have evolved around church life for centuries have been utilized by satan to steal this intimacy, relationship, and love affair with our First Love, the Lord Jesus, that we have always been meant to have. Consider that if Jesus is the Bridegroom as the Bible declares, shouldn't we as the bride know what He looks, sounds, and even smells like? ...His eye and skin color, hair, the way He looks at you, His attire, disposition...just like the descriptive knowledge and picture you always have and behold of your natural spouse whom you obviously know most intimately. Again, imagine having the most extensive "bucket list," an intensely fulfilling resume of adventures, yet continuously sharing in all these abundant life moments with your First Love and closest, real friends.

While I was concealing my treasured experiences with the Lord from Stacey, she was turning to her parents, who are both believers, as well as two of the Methodist pastors. Again, one of the pastors told her that I read the Bible too literally. The other, with whom I attended a small group lunch study, said he did not believe in healing (although that soon changed). I had shared with Stacey how my friend Mike prayed in tongues, and she had, without my knowledge, read some of my emails to Mike, desperately looking for answers, because again, she found all of this to be most troubling. That prompted a lunch meeting on December the 8th with a family member at Wendy's. I know the date because Mike had encouraged me to get a journal and document everything that was happening with me.

The family friend showed up at Wendy's with a Bible in his hand. I ordered a coffee and listened. Interestingly, he cited a couple of passages in the Bible to try to show me that speaking in tongues was not for today. It is also most interesting to note that I had previously had a lunch meeting with another pastor where we worshipped, and he told me that one of the passages we had discussed at the end of Mark was not in all manuscripts and probably wasn't meant to be in the Bible.

I left both of these meetings rather upset. I was so excited about what was happening to me and wanted to share it, but my family members and church pastors weren't ready to believe everything I had shared. (I had wrongly assumed that seasoned, professional clergy could identify with what I had shared with them.) Yet, while a little taken back, the love I was feeling during this life experience could in no way change what I now KNEW (18) through experience, nor could it shake the joy that had saturated every cell of my body. My wife was confused and upset about what was going on, as I was seemingly some nutcase walking around the house all hours of the night. Well, that night was different.

TICKER TAPE NIGHT VISION

What happened next was exhilarating, far beyond my ability to articulate. I went to bed, was lying on my back, with my hands clasped behind my head, closed my eyes, and Papa (Father God) came again. As before, I had the same feelings of love with the vibrations going all throughout my entire body. Then a ticker tape appeared to me just like you would see in a dream, except I was wide awake. That's an understatement! It was a passage in the Bible, referred to as The Great Commission, moving from right to left through my mind, (Right to left is backwards for the Western mind set, making me wonder about God's intent with a seemingly Hebraic path.)

"And He said to them, 'Go into all the world and preach the gospel to every creature. He who believes and is baptized will be saved; but he who does not believe will be condemned. And these signs will follow those who believe: In My name they will cast out demons; they will speak with new tongues; they will take up serpents; and if they drink anything deadly, it will by no means hurt them; they will lay hands on the sick, and they will recover.'" (19)

I got up out of bed and walked around the house for a few hours praising God and thanking Him for what had just occurred. These Scriptures were a destiny message for me...from the Father and to His son. Wow! I so craved to hear from Him and wanted more and more...and more. What else was so unusual was that this passage had been shared with me by two people: one, in a poor attempt to tell me that speaking in tongues was not for today, and a pastor, who stated that this passage was likely erroneously included in God's Word. To the contrary, on the night of December 8, 2002, Papa intervened and not only helped answer these questions, but made it emphatically clear that this was for me, and now even a part of me, resonating through every fiber of my being. I walked around the house pondering all of this, and then returned to bed for maybe a couple hours of sleep before heading to the office. However, when my head hit the pillow, I soon realized Father had something else for me, and the vision, vibrations, and His love continued with another Scripture:

"For by grace you have been saved through faith, and that not of yourselves; it is the gift of God, not of works, lest anyone should boast." (20)

It took me a few years to understand why the Lord had given me this Scripture until one day I asked Him (again) and he directed me to the following:

"But the manifestation of the Spirit is given to each one for the profit of all: for to one is given the word of wisdom through the Spirit, to another the word of knowledge through the same Spirit, to another faith by the same Spirit, to another gifts of healings by the same Spirit, to another the working of miracles, to another prophecy, to another discerning of spirits, to another different kinds of tongues, to another the interpretation of tongues. But one and the same Spirit works all these things, distributing to each one individually as He wills." (21)

As I meditated on this, I realized that He had given me the gift of faith found in verse nine of the passage on what we refer to as the manifestation or spiritual gifts. (22) The Ephesians passage had other meanings for me as well. I remember creating a diagram regarding salvation that came to me and Ephesians 2:8 was the part of that graphic that I used a few times teaching Sunday school. I don't think I slept that night, yet again I went to work so high on God, so full of Life, and feeling powerfully refreshed.

JOHNNY AND THE HEALING ANGEL

A day or two after this I experienced what would be one of the most invigorating days of my existence. As I was driving to the office, a feeling came over me regarding Johnny, a man who had attended the 112 Group and lived about forty-five minutes north of Shreveport. A year earlier I had read an article on the front page of the paper recognizing him for an act of bravery as a US

Marine during the Vietnam War. Johnny worked in para rescue and was stationed on the Island of Guam. There were some caves and tunnels on the island that descended 300 feet straight down and curved outward to the ocean. Some teenagers had tied a rope around a tree at the mouth of the cave and were rappelling down to the ocean. Their ropes were at least a hundred feet too short. They unfortunately lacked the strength to climb back to the top, fell and perished on the rocks below. In response to the teenagers' screams for help the Marines were called into action, arriving rapidly on the scene by helicopter. Johnny tied off a rope around the same tree and descended into the cave at a fearless pace, swaying back and forth while shoving off of the walls with his boots. He hadn't made it very far when his head hit a stalagmite which pierced him and knocked him unconscious. He fell two hundred feet to the rocks below. Fellow Marines recovered him somehow and medevac'd him to the hospital. A once tall, strong, former Golden Gloves boxer, Johnny now withered away in a bed, in a comatose state for nine months, until the Lord awakened him one day. Following a brain operation, Johnny was honorably discharged. According to The Shreveport Times newspaper article Johnny was the only prehumously-awarded recipient of the Medal of Heroism. His honoring came as he lay near death in the hospital bed. Nobody had given him much hope of survival.

Shift forward to mid-December. While driving to work the Holy Spirit put him on my heart, as I felt led to pray for his complete healing. I called him and he told me about debilitating arthritis resulting from his accident on Guam. He welcomed me to come pray for him. I hung up and called Mike, but he didn't immediately feel as strongly as I did. So, as I parked my car Mike suggested that I ask the Lord for a sign so I would know for sure. As I walked from my car to the office, dressed in my suit and carrying my briefcase, I walked downtown on the main thoroughfare, only a block from my destination. Suddenly I heard powerful singing coming from around the corner, yet it was converging on the path I was traversing.

The beautiful singing reminded me of Josh Groban singing in his native foreign language or some other, and it was loud -- so loud it could have been heard from a mile away. Imagine this bizarre sight for a Monday morning in a downtown business district. As the man from whom the singing was coming approached my path, I tried to speak with him, but we only made eye contact (I will never forget the look he gave me.), and he kept on singing. He looked to be in his thirties and not particularly well dressed, reminding me of a homeless person. I also remember his off-brand sneakers. He continued singing while he made a right turn on the sidewalk of Texas Street and kept going as I entered the building. I was blown away by this and quickly called Mike from my office to tell him what I had seen and heard. He said, "Dude, that was an angel, singing in his angelic tongue." I had already figured that out and knew that my sign I asked for had been granted, and we were supposed to pray for Johnny.

Elated, I then asked Mike if he wanted to go with me. He said that he still felt weird about this, so I told him to ask the Lord for his own sign. I also reminded him of how the Lord sent them out in pairs to "heal the sick, cleanse the lepers, and raise the dead." (23) Two is better than one. Mike was thinking the same thing as he asked the Lord to show him the number "two" spelled out when he opened his Bible. He opened his Bible and sure enough the first thing he saw was the word "two" illuminated. Mike, having admitted he was uneasy about this exploit, said that he did this fully 33 times and got the word "two" every time. 33 times seemed adequate for Mike (That's hilarious!) because he called me back and agreed that we would make the northbound 45-minute drive after work together and pray for Johnny. I called Johnny and he was thrilled that we were coming. Interestingly, I recently had a friend remind me that we are not called to pray for the sick, but rather to heal them! (24)

Johnny's house was about a quarter-mile deep in the woods off a country road, surrounded by old, towering pine trees. We were drawn to pray for him in these woods that felt so alive, so surreal, so heavenly... After trekking maybe 75 meters into the forest, we found – no, we felt the place for our mission of obedience. A sense of purpose filled us just as the musty, piney smells of the forest, the weight of its history and natural glory filled us – everything made sense, felt right. We huddled into a tight circle, rays of light penetrating the treetops like a heavenly host, and we began to pray. A dizzying flood of foreign words I did not understand gushed out of Mike and Johnny. They cried out in tongues, an experience I was not yet terribly familiar with but would soon come to know. I prayed all the harder in my own tongue. Then I heard Johnny, in English now, crying out "Heal the pain! Heal the pain!" I opened my eyes. Johnny was still speaking in tongues. What came next I will always remember. With my eyes closed again, I heard the rustling of dry leaves. It grew louder, approaching. We all opened our eyes and saw something magnificent – a wonder. A half-dozen or more white-tailed deer were circling us, seemingly with great purpose. The gentle thuds of their hooves upon the ground and leaves as they circled enthralled me. The awe was indescribable. Time seemed to stop and, our circle seemed to be the center of the universe for a lingering moment. I glanced at Mike and Johnny as they glanced at me as if we were saying "This is crazy, right?" And yet it did not feel that way, but to the contrary it felt like the way things were really meant to be. And then Johnny stood up, as straight as the pine trees around us. He was not crippled by arthritis. He was no longer hobbled. The deer had disappeared, and Johnny shadow-boxed with elation, his Golden-Gloves boxing days coming back to him, the vigor of life returned to him. Johnny was healed. We took half an hour to discuss this miraculous event, still in a stupor. Finally, we all embraced, and then Mike and I departed. Like the old days when I would fly 9-hour night missions in B-52s and then critique the mission, we recounted, analyzed and obsessed over all the details of the event that had unfolded before us. We had landed and accomplished the mission. It would not be the last and the details might help reveal the path to the next adventure.

One thing that Mike and I realized was that we both had actually interpreted tongues. This was one of the nine manifestation gifts of the Spirit. (25) I watched Johnny's lips as he prayed in the Spirit, in a heavenly tongue, but what I clearly heard was plain English. His lips were not even in sync with the sounds I heard in English. I thought it unusual that I had interpreted tongues before I spoke in tongues. I later learned that when you are functioning in the spiritual gifts, there is no effort; it just happens. If you spend time thinking about it, you are engaging your brain and will likely come out of the Spirit. On the matter of deer running around us, something I will cover later, it is scriptural and had a huge meaning for me regarding my destiny and this encounter. I drove home and thought about all of this for most of the night. My adrenaline level was so high, I knew that sleep would be impossible, but I was ecstatic about my life as a newfound nocturnal *flaneur*. (Flaneur is French for someone who takes long walks and ponders things.)

THE FINAL NIGHT VISION

So, it should be no surprise that the next several days I slept very little. The excitement about everything that had been materializing in my life was still so overwhelming that all I wanted to do was spend time with the Lord. Nothing at all was more important to me -- not eating, going to bed at night, sports, or anything else. Stacey, on the other hand, was at her wit's end. Then on Friday night, December the 21st of 2002, at precisely 2 a.m., the 40th day of this encounter, I laid down in bed. Within a minute or so of lying on my back and putting my head on the pillow the Lord came again for the last time during this season. The same incredible vibrations of life began again energizing every cell in my body from head to toe. His warmth and love saturated me so strongly that words can't really describe what was going on while I lay there on my back. I was so engrossed in this wonderful feeling, most curious about what was going to happen next, when I started to see a swirling blinding light. The best way to describe this is that it was basically a spiral that was swirling (pictured on the cover of this book), except much more intense. The light was so bright that I could barely keep my eyes closed, like my eyelids were almost burning or about to catch on fire. Yet I did not want to open my eyes because I knew that would stop the vision. So, for about five minutes, I watched this swirling light go around and around while the intoxicating oscillations in every cell of my body continued. To this day I have never felt so intensely loved; His warmth was so strong that I never wanted it to end. The vision did end, and I got up out of bed and walked around the house all night talking to the Lord and praising Him for being my God and for revealing Himself to me, His son. I had met Light, Life, and Love, Papa my Father. After several hours I went back to bed hoping that when I put my head on the pillow and closed my eyes that I would encounter Him again. Sadly, that would be the last of the visions of this forty-day season. Still, I awakened the next morning feeling so empowered and special that I could tackle any problem that the world threw at me.

The next day, Saturday, I remember walking around the parking lot at Target contemplating everything that had happened in my life for the last 40 days. I was not very good at engaging my wife, or anyone else in conversation because I was so engulfed with what had happened, walking and day-dreaming in an attention deficit disorder type of state, literally still feeling like I was in another realm, heavenly, and yet nearly unaware of my worldly surroundings. While Stacey was inside the store, I paced the parking lot, thinking about what had occurred the prior night, when the Lord spoke to me and told me that that was the end of all this for now. It took me years to understand what had transpired. Essentially, Father God had shown Himself to me as a blinding light, so powerful and full of love, and He was extending an invitation to me to be His son, His inheritance created in His image and likeness...to truly know Him in the most intimate way imaginable, to converse with Him daily, even continuously, and to have companionship as His friend, and offspring, and even to see His Son face to face as Moses, Abraham, and others had. Wow!

After I experienced these forty days with the Lord, I spent a considerable amount of time in the Bible as I recalled and reflected upon others similarly having forty-day God seasons. I learned then that often when God wanted to prepare and/or test someone for His purposes, He did this over forty days: Noah's life was radically altered by 40 days of rain. Moses spent 40 days on Mt. Sinai. The spies were renewed by 40 days in the Promised Land. David had a 40-day challenge by Goliath. Elijah was transformed when God gave him 40 days of strength from a single meal. The entire city of Nineveh was reshaped when God gave the people 40 days to change. Jesus was empowered after 40 days in the wilderness, and the disciples were especially transfigured by 40 days with the Lord Jesus after the resurrection. The most exhilarating emphasis on all of this is the invitation to be God's seemingly most treasured, favorite son or daughter, that there is nothing more important for Him than to spend time and truly, intimately know us and share in all that we do. For me, I find Him and come to know Him more closely in the simplicity of living life without conditions or rules, but rather by following the nudging, subtle cravings, and guidance from within...just living life by doing what I enjoy, and seeking, thanking, praising, acknowledging Him in both the bad and the good times.

STACEY ENTERS THE KINGDOM OF GOD

Another night of me up all night followed by my wandering around the Target parking lot talking to God prompted some difficult conversation with Stacey. That evening we sat down in the living room, both in tears, as I spent at least two hours filling her in on the concluding events of this forty-day encounter. Like me, until I was forty years old, Stacey did not understand that she could have a personal relationship with the Lord. I just recently had a conversation with a family member who was talking to me about all the different nations and the different religions that the nations embraced. He said that, basically, we all have our own beliefs and some day we will find out who is right. Well, this statement disturbed me, even saddened me about his spiritual walk; it had become abundantly clear to me that Jesus did not come to bring a religion or a philosophy, but a relationship and a way of life founded upon love, or Love, the Person. I openly challenged all of the other religions and their gods: "Can you talk to him and hear back? Can you know your god like you know your wife? Can you tell me what he looks like?" I desperately wanted Stacey to have a truly meaningful relationship with the one, true God.

When Stacey came to the realization that I was not lying or exaggerating, that I really cared for her deeply, and that I wanted her to have what I was experiencing, she changed in a powerfully good way. That night Stacey decided that she wanted all of God. The next day, Sunday, was a phenomenal day for the whole family. I was teaching tenth grade Sunday school which our oldest two daughters attended. Our other two daughters were with us but were in a class for younger kids. On the way to church, a white dove (white like your bed sheets) flew in front of us and guided us part way to church. I was so on fire from these experiences that I taught the class this time while the co-teacher mostly listened as I talked about having a relationship with the Holy Spirit. After class, I pulled aside the co-teacher and explained everything that had happened to me. I then, overzealously, tried to see him filled with the Lord's Holy Spirit by the laying on of hands, which I had read about in the Bible. (26) (As I reflect upon this it reminds me of the movie, *Nacho Libre*, where actor Jack Black snuck up on his wrestler friend and water baptized him without his consent.) I don't know why, but I turned the lights out in the room before I laid hands on him which angered him, since he believed that he received everything that he needed when he was born again. We debated one another until it was time for the contemporary church service. Just before the service, while seated, the Lord spoke to me and told me that Stacey was about to give her life to Him. So, I quickly told Stacey and our four daughters to move to the front row, and I went up and asked the pastor to make sure that he offered an invitation at the end of the service. (My actions here do exhibit, to some degree, my spiritual immaturity by trying to control the situation, rather than by trusting the Holy Spirit to set things in the proper order.) The minister, a wonderful man of God, looked perplexed and replied that he always extended an invitation. Sure enough, he gave a message based upon John 3:16 and, at the conclusion, Stacey came forth and told everyone that she was giving her life to Jesus. While I was so emotional about this incredible morning something of note happened as the service ended. We mingled afterwards, and I spoke to a man I'd never met. As we spoke his cheeks became rosy, then red. A deep, beet redness filled his face in the most unnatural way. Sweat poured out of him in a deluge. Time seemed to stop around us as he opened his mouth. No words came out, no reply to our conversation – just a roar, guttural, deep, and animalistic like that of a lion. Even his eyes flashed a predatory, hateful look. I felt a chill, like I was being hunted, like something wanted to consume me. satan sensed we belonged to God and no longer him. I did not waver. Then, everything was back to normal. I nervously exchanged niceties before peeling us away from him and exiting the building. Stacey and I were elated, now walking in spiritual unity, together divinely restored from darkness to light, man and woman as one, in the image and likeness of our Creator, as it was intended by our Father from the beginning.

I then explained and showed her in the Scriptures what happened in Acts 2, and that if she wanted to have the fullness of the Holy Spirit, I would pray with her for that. We did. Within about two weeks she was praying by herself in her shoe closet when, suddenly, she started singing in an angelic tongue. She was just moving her lips, not trying to sing anything, but the Spirit gave her utterance, as the Bible reads, in beautiful song. (27) Once that happened there were spiritual blessings that flowed generationally to our children. Stacey started having prophetic dreams EVERY night, for a season, as did the kids. We bought Stacey a pen with a lightbulb on the end of it and a diary to record her dreams. One night she woke up in the middle of the night to write down three dreams; about an hour later she woke up and wrote down another four dreams. She would go on to soon fill four diaries with nothing but dreams from the Lord.

So now Stacey was beginning to have a relationship with Jesus. When she spoke in tongues for the first time, a season began for her to speak with God just like having a conversation with me or anybody else, literally. She was now having an encounter just like I had for the last forty days. There were a few days when she would go into the living room and converse back and forth with God for hours. She also had her spiritual eyes opened and saw things in the spirit realm as well, both good and bad. As heaven is in our midst, we are surrounded by angels, demons, the saints that have gone on before us, etc., all of which we have been called to see with our natural open eyes, if we would only believe and practice exercising our spiritual senses. There are many examples of this in the Bible; perhaps most notable are the Old Testament references to seer prophets and their spiritual endeavors.

In the ensuing months if I sensed that someone needed healing for something in their body, I would ask Stacey if she would pray and tell me what she heard. I asked her what *she* was hearing because during this time of her life her ability to hear God seemed so incredibly easy for her that I was awestruck. Generally, we got the same response for those whom she prayed about: that if he or she believes, they will be healed. (28) When partnering with Stacey during this season, my faith rose dramatically when she told me that those who believed would be healed. I felt so tremendously inspired while praying for these folks. There was a season of several months that began with praying for the man in the coma, that every person that we prayed for was healed, provided they believed that

God would heal them. We witnessed some incredible miracles, but we also were discouraged while praying for some. I recall praying for a worship leader that had Tourette's syndrome, and I knew that he would be healed if only he believed. I think I was still praying in the King James which really weirded him out. The next Sunday I asked him if we could pray for him again, and he said no. This really troubled me because I felt so strongly that he and anybody could have their healing if they wanted it, and I had wrongly supposed that of all people, employed church staffers understood God's ways of His kingdom. With others I would try to educate them on how Jesus is the same yesterday, today, and forever (29), but I ran into a lot of people who had embraced dispensationalism or secessionist theology. It wasn't necessarily their fault -- they had just been in this place for so long without really experiencing Jesus or His love. Some believed, basically, that God either stopped performing miracles at the end of the book of Acts or that He only did them during certain seasons or dispensations, but not today. Still, the miracles that we saw were incredible. For example, we prayed for about a dozen people who had pain in their bodies, and ALL of them were healed. What made this so exciting was simply that God wanted to use ordinary people like us. For the next six months we did not personally know of anyone else who was praying for people like we were, (mostly following the model set forth by Jesus, the disciples, and others in the gospels and book of Acts), as we had not yet met them.

Interestingly, I recall that during these months I fasted regularly and ritualistically (Unfortunately doing most things ritualistically bears little fruit.) in an attempt to starve my "unbelief" as the Scriptures read. While I have not fasted for some time, I still believe that this practice often made me more in tune with my spiritual senses, in tune with God, and enhanced my faith. The disciples were not able to cast out a deaf and dumb spirit so they asked of the Lord, and He replied after He cast the demonic spirit out, "This kind can come out by nothing but prayer and fasting." (30)

MEMORABLE SUPERNATURAL DAYS DURING THE ENCOUNTER

One morning driving to the office, Mike told me over the phone that he felt the Lord wanted me to pray for someone dear to us. This person was in a state of depression, and satan's plan for him was to commit suicide. For about a month, every time I thought about him, I prayed in English and in tongues against this spirit of suicide. The last day, I was driving my vehicle, praying in the Spirit for him, when a blackbird flew from way up in the sky, out of nowhere, straight into the grill of my truck, while going about sixty-five miles per hour. At that moment I received a revelation that this spirit of death had been defeated / killed, and I no longer needed to pray for the young man.

Having never experienced the supernatural before my encounter, I was overzealous in wanting to share too much with just about everyone that I knew, of what was occurring. That's, again, a huge understatement. Still, I desperately wanted others to see how real God is. I wrongly believed that my testimonies of the supernatural, the healings, having seen an angel, deer running around us, and other things of God we experienced, would point and lead everyone to Jesus. I so desired to see lost (I think of these now as pre-Christians or better yet, friends.) or worldly people hear how powerful and loving our God really is. I recall sharing these things with a co-worker and another gentleman over lunch, separately. On both occasions I felt interrupted by the strongest sensation over my nose and mouth that became painful and worsened the more I shared. This made me try even harder because I thought satan was trying to prevent me from helping them. When I shared this with Mike the next day, he heard the word "bridle" in the Spirit. The Lord was trying to warn me about "casting pearls before swine" by bridling me. I knew this was the truth and quickly learned my lesson. The Lord said, "Do not give what is holy to the dogs; nor cast your pearls before swine, lest they trample them under their feet, and turn and tear you in pieces." (31) While this Scripture seems harsh and even unkind it is important to note how our God desires that all people come to the saving knowledge of Him and that none perish. (32) The Father has a plan and time to draw and bring all of us who accept Him unto Himself yet until then (except for those, mostly children, below their age of accountability) we belong to satan and his "dogs and swine." (33) The point He was trying to teach me was that I needed to use discernment with both content and to whom I directed my faith. Today I can't help but break out in laughter every time I reflect upon those lessons which were very serious at the time.

Another couple of important points to make note of is that, while the supernatural miracles of heaven/God are necessary for the most effective power evangelism, we should be winning souls by the power of the cross and the story of what Christ did for all humanity on that day. Secondly, there are many revelations of the cross; one, importantly to me, is a picture of communion with God first and foremost (the vertical part), yet the horizontal piece with Jesus' outstretched arms speaks to a needed communion that we must have with each other. The Lord had paired me with Mike in this season because we all have blind sides and therefore needed one another in order to function fully as Father had ordained us to. Had I not known about the bridle, for example, I may have caused great harm to others as well as myself.

THE SHOE STORE
IN THE MALL

One of the most memorable days of my forty-day experience was on a Saturday when Stacey and I went to Mall St. Vincent in Shreveport to buy her a pair of shoes. I had not slept at all the prior night, but I was so fully energized by His love, joy, and life, that I felt great. We were in the shoe store for at least several hours. I don't think that we bought any shoes or even tried anything on. Instead, we spent the whole time talking to complete strangers. Oddly enough, people would be walking past the store from the main thoroughfare of the mall and want to come inside to talk to us. It was as if we were supernaturally magnetized so that people were drawn to us, and the well of living water that we carried was released to them. Stacey and I would talk to an individual or a couple for twenty or thirty minutes and then another stranger would come. We couldn't leave the store. These were mostly people that we had never seen before. We just loved on them and listened, answered their questions, and smiled with great joy the whole time.

On Christmas Eve, the stock market closed at lunch time and everyone in the office started to leave to be with their families. Out of character for me (and most brokerage offices), a party animal guy who had lived on the edge for so long, I spoke to every person in the office before I left and gave them a heartfelt hug. I wanted to love on everybody. I remember some of the brokers being rather stiff but warmed up to me in response to my kindness. I even did this with my boss who I could tell was really touched by my actions during this Christmas season. Everyone knew without any doubt that Jesus had touched me. Love really does conquer all.

When I look back at some of my life accomplishments before I was in Christ, the thrill of victory in winning a foot race, beating name brand elitists in track and cycling, while setting course, school, or facility records in the process; there was such a rush with many of these milestones. Even my hedonistic exploits in college life and while playing rugby had huge highs, but ultimately left me with shallow fading memories, sometimes a conviction of error, and unfulfilled emptiness in my heart. In direct contrast to these worldly endeavors I cannot describe adequately with words how over the top, fulfilling, and joyful this experience with the Lord made me feel, live, and cherish. I wouldn't trade one day of my encounter for any of the aforementioned experiences before I met Him.

Jesus is the coolest, most radical man to ever walk the earth, sacrificially serving all humanity and I yearn each day to know, follow, and experience Him. His indescribable love and abundant life for me awaits.

PART II

DISCIPLESHIP: FROM THE ENCOUNTER UNTIL NOW

HUNGRY FOR GOD'S WORD

After Stacey had come into the Kingdom the Father began to put an enormous hunger for His Word into our hearts. We went through about a six-month season of reading the Bible every night after work until bedtime, getting up early to read, and spending most of the weekend in His timeless Book. We simply could not get enough of it. We realized that we were getting a late start in life, and really did not know what was in the Bible. The Lord gave us the craving to ingest His Word for hours and hours at a time. To this day as we continue to feast on His living daily Bread, the more we understand, the more we realize how little we know and how much more there is to know about Jesus and His kingdom. The Bible illuminated and came alive to us during this time as the Holy Spirit brought forth revelation and understanding. Where before I was hesitant to read the Bible because it did not make much sense to me, suddenly it was active and energetic -- Spirited. There were quite a few Scriptures that illuminated to me with special meaning. I could easily list dozens of Scriptures and passages that became seemingly eternally important, like this one, for example, that addresses this subject. "The Word of God is quick (alive) and powerful, and sharper than any two-edged sword, piercing even to the division of soul and spirit, and of joints and marrow, and is a discerner of the thoughts and intents of the heart (34)." I've figured that it takes me about seventy hours to read the Bible: fifty for the Old Testament and twenty for the New Testament. There were several occasions during this season I would come home from work on Friday and we would read the entire New Testament before going back to work on Monday. With each passing day our learning and understanding increased, as did our appetite. We simply could not get enough of this spiritual food during this time of our lives.

GETTING GROUNDED IN THE WORD AND PRAYING FOR FRIENDS AND ACQUAINTANCES

Stacey and I had a newfound boldness and courage to share the fullness of God, from a fresh perspective, with everyone that we knew. We wanted each person that was open to the things of the Spirit to encounter all of this for themselves, as we had. We would have people over to the house and pray for them to be filled with the Holy Spirit, to have a magnificent, discernible encounter with God through His Holy Spirit, just like we read about in Acts 2. We saw so much of a very real, supernatural God and the overwhelming saturation of His presence during these meetings. We wanted others to experience how tangible our God really is.

We remained at the same mainstream denominational church that we had been going to for nine years even though they expressly did not emphasize the gifts of the Holy Spirit that they once had flourished in years ago -- they look down upon this emphasis even more now. We simply wanted to be obedient to God's will and were not leaving there until He gave us direction. This happened much later than I thought it would, but about nine months after Stacey was born again we felt like we were clearly supposed to move to a local Assembly of God fellowship under the direction of our new Sunday school teacher, a surgeon who everyone addressed as "Dr. Byrd." I had written Dr. Byrd a letter expressing an interest in meeting him. After a few days, he called me late in the afternoon. When I heard the phone ring, I knew by the Spirit that he was on the other end, so instead of having the call go through the switchboard, I answered it, and immediately felt a connection. We were there about two years under the tutelage of Dr. Byrd, we believe to get a stronger foundation in God's Word. Dr. Byrd was a disciple and personal friend of Andrew Wommack who had a huge teaching and healing ministry in

Colorado. We soon thereafter had a dream and further guidance which led us to The Faith Church north of Shreveport. The Lord had shown us in the dream that we would be there for a season as well, we believe mainly for the purpose of growing in spiritual discernment. Our family later worshipped at another local house of God in Shreveport called The Christian Center where we had a special emphasis on learning how to hear God's voice. Ultimately, we were led into home fellowship and discipleship where we are now, yet we have been discipled / fathered in more of a family / home worship style atmosphere most of the entire time since we experienced our encounters.

Humorously I recall that when I found out that Andrew Wommack traveled regularly to Venezuela, I became overzealous in attempting to team up with him, a man I did not know personally, because I wrongly thought that my dreams and visions had to be tied to what he was doing. I wrote a letter to him, and when I did not get a response, I repeatedly called his personal secretary to let her know (in error) of my divine call to assist their ministry efforts. While not yet part of Papa's plans for me, this experience illustrates the need for a spiritual father and his nurturing discipleship.

MANIFESTATION OF THE VENEZUELA NIGHT VISION

Mike and I had maintained a close friendship, and he eventually introduced me to a man named Mickey who mentored me for about a year and became another good friend. The first time that I met Mickey he gave me some Scriptures for my destiny which he heard while praying, from Luke 4 and Isaiah 46, that really touched me. The freshness, comfort, and awakening that came that day really inspired me. A prophetic word from the Lord delivered by a believer should confirm something that we already know. There was no doubt in this case. Mickey and Mike soon became business partners, and we all started getting together, along with others, at their office during lunch, to pray, seek the Lord, and see what the Holy Spirit wanted to do with everyone present. During the first several meetings God's presence was incredible. Mike received a revelation that at the end of one meeting I was to pray over him in tongues, something I had never done before. Sure enough, the Holy Spirit came over me, I opened my mouth and spoke, and out it came: an unknown heavenly tongue. The exhilarating feeling of God's goodness all over my body made it easy to do this....all that I had to do was open my mouth and speak. Mickey was present and gave an interpretation that was a personal message for Mike. We saw a refreshing, Spirit-directed / ordered participation from most of the people who came, and several were filled with the Lord's Holy Spirit. (35)

It was during this time that the vision I had about Venezuela began to line up and take shape. The initial connection to Venezuela came about one

Sunday when Stacey and I were already in the car leaving church with our four daughters. They were whining about wanting to eat lunch when I was prompted by the Holy Spirit to go back inside to hear a gentleman talk about Methodist missions. He was the state director for Louisiana, and we were the only people who cared to show up for this divine appointment. He connected me with some people from Alabama, a Venezuelan named Zabdiel who often traveled back and forth from Alabama to Venezuela, and a powerful man of God named Jesse Stokely. Mr. Stokely was from the family that canned and distributed Stokley-Van Camp beans and other vegetables, and he was the project chief consultant to bring Gatorade to commercialization. His family work experience and educational background was a lead in to one of the largest mission efforts in the world from his home and port in Houston. I had felt led by the Holy Spirit to write a letter to Mr. Stokely about how I felt we were called to Venezuela. About three weeks went by before I received a phone call from an elated Jesse Stokely who said that he had been in prayer and the Lord told him that we would be mightily used in that region. He wanted to help. Ultimately, Mickey, Mike, and I flew to Venezuela, via Houston so that we could meet Jesse. We hung out for about three hours with him and had so much fun visiting that we would have missed our flight had we not run the whole way to the gate. We then spent eight days in Venezuela, deep in the jungle on the large Caura River. We went up and down this massive waterway treating native tribes with antibiotics and vitamins and providing clothing. We also told them about Jesus and the revelation of how we got there. Because of the relational foundation that Zabdiel had laid and nurtured here, we were especially received by the natives. We could all feel such a sincere affinity for one another. One of the days we rented a Cessna 172 and flew more than two hours to visit Angel Falls -- undiscovered until 1957 and breathtakingly beautiful. Also noteworthy was our travel one day when suddenly Zabdiel felt prompted to pull off the road and drive a dirt path back to a sensationally alluring lake where I was water baptized in the name of Jesus. I had felt that this was the time and place, and I had not yet had a biblical baptism (36) that occurred after salvation. An eagle flew overhead when I was submerged as we faced a herd of water buffalo. This whole experience seemed heavenly, so surreal—like we were in a glorified realm the whole time, and with the animal kingdom groaning, travailing, awaiting for real men of God to manifest themselves, subdue the earth, take dominion, and step into our God given mandate.

I described to Zabdiel the place that I had seen in my first night vision, and he drove us straight to the cemetery, just as it was in the vision, with the white wall and mango orchard behind it. We walked around inside it and sure enough, there was a tomb stone statue of Jesus with a fence around it. I had several dreams while I was there regarding returning in the future to share God's word and help evangelize these wonderful people. The Lord showed me that a great harvest would take place there, with healing and deliverance of His people. In one of the dreams I was picking up potatoes, which speaks of this harvest, and shaking black ants out of the potatoes into the nearby river to be washed away. In another, I was standing next to the statue of Jesus while a long line of Venezuelan men was running and hurdling the fence to get to us.

DALLAS HEALING TRIP

Back in Louisiana, as I was getting up to go to work my cell phone rang and it was Mike. He had a friend in Texas that was close to a family whose son had been diagnosed with terminal cancer and didn't have long to live. The boy was named Cade and he was only two years old. Mike told me that he had been praying and felt that the Lord wanted several of us to drive to the hospital in Dallas and pray for him. He told me not to worry about my work, that God would cover us while we were gone. So, Mike, Mickey, Mike's friend Ken, and a man I had met in Sunday school named Mark all met at a truck stop on Interstate 20 in Shreveport. I drove us all to the hospital in Dallas. We had wonderful conversation along the way, mostly the sharing of personal testimonies of how the Lord had been working in our lives. We then prayed and felt that the Lord had shown us a few things regarding our venture.

We got to the hospital, parked, and soon found Cade's room. His parents and grandparents were there, and I believe that the nurses let all of us hang out in his room because there was little to no hope for him. We told the family, whom none of us knew, that we felt that we were sent ones on a mission, and we were thrilled to be there, despite the circumstances. We got permission to lay hands on Cade and pray for him. I recall that I had just begun to pray in the Spirit and did so as I put my hands on him and prayed softly. Everyone else put their hands on my back, and we fervently prayed for his healing. There was a tangible presence from God that was so strong; He was most assuredly there with us. Just like I had read in the Scriptures countless times when Jesus prayed for the sick, I too had compassion come upon me as I beheld this small sickly two-year old. I also recall a conviction from the power of the Holy Spirit where Cade's grandfather openly confessed some things about himself to all of us, which had been held back for a long time. This was a catalyst for a real sense of emotional healing for the whole family. We left there knowing that we had been obedient to God's will in this divine appointment, that whatever happened was in His hands. We drove to a Mexican restaurant in Dallas and had a great time; we were all so full of joy during our lunch conversation and later as we made the three-hour trek back to Shreveport. When I came into the office the next day, I discovered, most unusually that I had not had a single call from the prior day while we were gone.

Our time with Cade was about a week prior to Thanksgiving. The family knew in their hearts that Cade had been healed, especially since his symptoms disappeared. They had the doctors run tests and confirmed that he was indeed, inexplicably to them, cancer free. When his physician asked that he stay for some more confirming tests, the family decided that was unnecessary and checked Cade out and took him home, just in time for this most meaningful season of thanksgiving. Interestingly, on Sunday in church they shared this wonderful testimony, and it caused a split with this mainstream denominational group of believers because many had been indoctrinated with a belief system that healing was not for today. Cade's family, however, KNEW differently! (37) Just recently we were sent an email from Cade, now 16 years old, posing with a large antlered white-tailed deer he shot during the week of Thanksgiving.

DISCIPLESHIP

Mickey and I soon became good friends. He invited me one day to have lunch with an acquaintance of his named Jack McClendon. Jack was the nephew of long time LSU head football coach, Charlie McClendon, known as "Charlie Mac." I remember well the Italian lunch Mickey, Jack, Mike, and I ate together. We had a wonderful meal, but I was really struck by our conversation with Jack who spoke to us in parables; I'm not exaggerating. This sounds hysterical, but at the time, I understood very little of what he talked about. With the conclusion of our lunch he held our hands, one at a time, and prayed for us. He asked that we open our eyes and look into his eyes while he vehemently prayed. There was clearly an impartation, a fear of the Lord, and immediately a love for each other.

About two weeks after our lunch I had an unforgettable dream. I was wading with my wife and four daughters in warm water that was up to my chest. I noticed a silver colored fish that was, I knew, about four pounds. While admiring the fish which was swimming around all of us, I put my hands into the water to pick him up, and he stuck his ventral fin into my thumb. It did not hurt at all. After a minute or so I pulled the fin out of my thumb and placed him back into the water. He continued to swim around us. I had the dream on March the 17th of 2004, and knew it had significant meaning for our family. I looked up the fish in a book and discovered that it was a Coho Salmon. This was unusual because I knew that we were in warm water, yet this was a cold-water fish. With some help from a friend named Ginny I soon had the interpretation of this dream. The fish was Jack McClendon and the Lord meant for him to be our spiritual father or mentor. I knew that he was the fish because of the silver color which matched the part of his hair on the sides where he wasn't bald. The ventral fin which he stuck in my thumb symbolized an apostolic or foundational impartation.

I learned this from the following scripture, "And He Himself gave some to be apostles, some prophets, some evangelists, and some pastors and teachers, for the equipping of the saints for the work of ministry for the edifying of the body of Christ, till we all come to the unity of the faith and of the knowledge of the son of God, to a perfect man, to the measure of the stature of the fullness of Christ; that we should no longer be children, tossed to and fro and carried about with every wind of doctrine, by the trickery of men, in the cunning craftiness of deceitful plotting, but, speaking the truth in love, may grow up in all things into Him who is the head -- Christ -- from whom the whole body, joined and knit together by what every joint supplies, according to the effective working by which every part does its share, causes growth of the body for the edifying of itself in love." (38) I've learned that the symbology of the hand in dreams generally stands for what is referred to as the five-fold ministry. (39)

The apostle is a master builder as represented by the thumb. Notice that the thumb can touch all the other fingers, gifts (people) to the body of Christ. The index finger represents the prophet by pointing to the future and knowing the end from the beginning (see Isaiah 46). The evangelist is the middle finger which is the longest and reaches out and brings in the new converts. The pastor is represented by the ring finger where the ring is symbolic of the shepherd in covenant with his flock, and the little finger is the teaching gift. This is the smallest finger but the only one small enough to fit in your ear, so while small, very important. Note that pastoring and teaching go together as evidenced by the absence of a comma after "pastor." The point of all this goes with the interpretation. You would think that Jack must have been an apostle, represented by the thumb in my dream, but upon further study and reflection / teaching, I believe that, while he functioned apostolically, his gift to the body was likely that of a prophet. The impartation into my thumb more represented the rendering / teaching of a much needed foundation in the things of the Lord. Even today I was reading in the Bible where Israel defeated the Canaanites and Perizzites and chopped the thumbs and big toes off Adoni-Bezek for having done the same himself to seventy kings. (40) Imagine the importance of our thumbs, or rather what life would be like without the use of them. So, the dream indicated that he was going to be leading our family through deep water, or the very deep things of the Lord. (41) I called him and shared the dream with this man who I had only ever met once. Admittedly, I felt intimidated by his spiritual authority when I shared the dream and interpretation with him. Of course, the Lord had already shown him, our new shepherd, this union of our families, but I had to come to him with this or he would otherwise be exerting control in the relationship.

We immediately started fellowshipping together. Jack and his wife Pat soon became a real spiritual father and mother to us, and we became the closest of friends. They discipled us just the way I'd imagined and read how Jesus shepherded the twelve, helping us to mature in Christ, but most importantly pointing us to Jesus. Just like in Paul's writings, we were called to follow and even imitate them with our spiritual walk. We did this wholeheartedly as we knew that was the Father's plan. Jack was available 24/7, especially if we wanted to go bass fishing. Jack and Patricia mentored our family for four years. I never really got the complete interpretation of the meaning of the four-pound fish in my dream until St. Patrick's Day, March 17 of 2008. On that day Jack fell over backwards in his driveway, knocked his head, and crossed over to the other realm awaiting him. He had recently shared a dream with family which revealed to him his own passing. The four-pound salmon represented precisely four years of friendship and fellowship from March 17, 2004, when I had the dream, until March 17 of 2008, to the day! Jack had an unforgettable sense of humor; the Lord as well, taking a man named McClendon home on St. Patty's Day.

We probably fished fifty times together, laughing and cutting up, talking about the Lord, and issues near and dear to our work and families. We went fishing on Sunday, the day before he left us. He was one of the best fishermen that I ever knew, and his sense of humor attracted everyone he came into contact with. He had several tackle boxes full of lures that must have easily weighed fifty pounds each. (Imagine a huge toy chest with hundreds of little toys / lures.) But what was so striking was that he only fished with hard baits. Even in the summer Louisiana heat when hard baits typically don't work, Jack would eventually tie one on and catch a pile of fish. Eerily, the first time he used a soft bait while fishing with me was that Sunday before he passed. It was as if he knew that would be the last opportunity for him to do that with me.

We were fishing on Caddo Lake, and that day he was more of a servant guiding me around while operating the trolling motor. He did not fish a whole lot that day, other than trying out some of my plastic frogs for the first time. I managed to catch three bass, the largest of which weighed about six and a half pounds. I later felt I heard that the fish was symbolic of Jack having taken me part way from a six to a seven. (In the Bible seven is God's number of perfection, and six is His number for humanism or carnality.) I shared the dream that I had about Jack at his funeral which his son Brad directed. During the funeral, a number of people kept hearing a train passing by, yet this was in the Spirit because there weren't any trains nearby. We believe that the sound of the train spoke of a coming move of God which Jack helped to found and nurture. About five months after the funeral I had a dream about his son, who was to be our new spiritual father.

Only after I had known Brad for several years did I feel loved by any man like I did when spending time with Jack. I tried to spend as much time as possible with him because the atmosphere of joy that encompassed him was incredibly addictive. I also felt selfishly that I had to be growing in the Lord when I hung out with him because he really was the closest representation of Jesus I had ever known. Several times during the four years I knew him, when I was having a bad day, he would know prior to any conversation, and show up in my office, usually in his favorite blue pants and red windbreaker, with an ear to ear grin on his face and something funny to say which would always make me laugh and uplift any poor mood. We were family. The last few months with him were extraordinarily special. The last word from the Lord which he gave me was, "reckless abandonment." *Go for it, no holding back, with any Divine inspiration, do not rely upon human reasoning, just act.*

DAVID MOVES TO SHREVEPORT

My brother David, eighteen months my junior, began to have a series of dreams of us playing golf and doing other recreational (spiritual re-creating) things together in Shreveport. He soon came down from Virginia for a visit and we met with Mickey in his office. Mickey spoke prophetically over David and he really got whacked by the Lord's Holy Spirit. At the time he had a sciatic nerve problem that restricted his range of motion and ability to walk or run. I scheduled a session with a man in East Texas named Randy who had a healing ministry through acupuncture. Forty needles and thirty minutes later he got up completely healed. We came home and did a twenty-mile bike ride together that afternoon! Shortly thereafter David bought a house in Shreveport and moved his family from northern Virginia.

David soon became involved with our home fellowship. One of the most exciting miracles that I have ever seen involved his oldest boy Dillon one evening at our house. Dillon was plagued with symptoms of autism; at times he did not engage people. Instead he would find coins or building blocks and spend an inordinate amount of time stacking and making rows of them in his own realm, oblivious to his surroundings. That ended when, one night, David and Jack prayed for Dillon, and he was delivered of an autism demon. Though he was only about two years old, Dillon could see the demon once it left him, in the spirit realm, and he jumped up and down on it, elated that this thing had left his body. He was completely healed that night.

WEDNESDAY LUNCH MEETINGS

The lunch meetings that Mickey, Mike, and I attended in their office were greatly enhanced once Jack entered the picture. Jack would pray in the morning and always knew what the Lord wanted to accomplish. He was the shepherd who understood the needs of his sheep. Generally, there was a very timely teaching, followed by prayer. During some of the meetings we experienced astoundingly supernatural things of God in His incredible presence. Jack brought order to these very diverse meetings. One time the Lord had us laughing uncontrollably for more than an hour whereby the Holy Spirit was delivering us with inner healing, and none of us could contain this most joyful roaring and howling. We all left there changed. Another time, the Lord led someone to wash another's feet. The following meeting quite a few people came who did not believe in the gifts of the Spirit, nor the supernatural, wanting to see signs that God was real, and the Lord did nothing. I believe that this occurred because it is 'by grace through faith' (Ephesians 2:8) that we are saved, not miracles. We just waited on Him in prayer for an hour before returning to work. Most noteworthy to me was that sometimes every person in the group would have something from the Lord that fit the message and was meant to be shared. This reminded me of the following, "How is it then, brethren? Whenever you come together, each of you has a psalm, has a teaching, has a tongue, has a revelation, has an interpretation. Let all things be done for edification." (42) We had several meetings where every person present, under the direction of the Holy Spirit participated just like this Scripture indicates, and everyone was indeed edified.

NEW SPIRITUAL FATHER IN THE LORD

On September 1st, 2008, a little more than five months after Jack's funeral, I had another unforgettably sensational dream. In the dream Brad McClendon (again, Jack's son) and I were riding in an orange / yellow mega truck, like you would see in a huge mining operation. Brad was driving and I was in the passenger seat up front.

There was another man sitting in the back of the truck who looked Native American. Riding in this monstrous earth moving vehicle, we pulled up to a gravel pit that had been converted into a landfill / junkyard. When I got out, I again noticed that the tires were so large that they went well over my head. Upon our arrival, Brad looked over at me sternly like I had some kind of inspiration or revelation, and asked, "What do you have?" After considering his question I knew that there was hidden treasure at this place in the gravel pit, so I jumped out and started picking up old metal furniture. As I shook the junky furniture, dated silver, gold, and nickel coins began to fly out everywhere. I picked them up and handed them to Brad. I then took the pieces of furniture and threw them into the truck cab because I knew that there was a lot more treasure in it that I had to shake out. One of the coins was a pre-1943 Mercury silver dime. All three of us then jumped back into the truck and left. The Indian man had driven up there with us, gotten out and watched, and returned with us, but never spoke a word the whole time. In the dream I also knew about this place from having been with Brad's father, Jack. I woke up and looked at the clock: 1:53 a.m.

I sent an email to Brad for help with the interpretation, which for the most part, was pretty self-explanatory. He said that the interpretation in a nutshell was, "trash to treasure." The Lord was going to show us things that at first glance might seem insignificant or of little value, but were actually of great importance, treasure. The Indian man in the dream was the Holy Spirit, the Teacher, our Comforter, and the best scout that a man could ever have. He was the Co-worker, in the dream, the One Father God sent after His Son Jesus ascended following His crucifixion, so that we could do the works that He did.

The large vehicle spoke of Brad's ministry. It was important that he was driving, and I was a passenger under his walk, or following him.

Although Brad would never tell me this, I was clearly supposed to support his ministry financially as evidenced by me giving him the coins and placing the metal furniture into the cab of the truck which represented his journey with God.

BREAKTHROUGH IN SOUTH AFRICA

During the next year I got to know Brad much better as we emailed and spoke on the phone periodically. Immediately from the start of our conversations Brad helped awaken me to a rudimentary understanding and recognition of how and when the Lord was speaking to me. The subtleties in this lifelong process involved discerning my soulish or humanistic thoughts and reasoning from His higher ways in the heavenlies. The difficulty in this for me was in the simplicity of heavenly communication directed to me and recognizing the Gift that resided within me. This likely appears to be ridiculously straightforward, but often just liking things or even people comes from divine inspiration from within. The joy that comes from this perpetual voyage of hearing and discerning His voice and feeling His presence is uplifting and addictive beyond words.

Stacey and I soon began to attend Morningstar conferences where Brad was a pastor. Shortly thereafter he invited me to go to South Africa with him, and after feeling that I was indeed supposed to go, I purchased a flight. A week or two before I departed for Johannesburg, at a home fellowship meeting at Brad's mom's house a man told me at the conclusion that something profound was going to occur while I was in Johannesburg. I told him that was odd because I would only be there to catch connecting flights: to Durban, and my return flight home.

On September 7th, 2009 I boarded a Delta flight for the sixteen-hour flight from Atlanta to "Jo-burg" where I would meet up with Brad at the airport. We had winds that were contrary to the normal jet stream, so I had to rush upon landing to get to the gate for the connecting flight. Even though I was thirty-five minutes early my seat had been given to someone else, and I was required to purchase another ticket for a later flight. This trip started out poorly as the lady I dealt with at the ticket window clearly had racial issues. After another ninety minutes I found Brad at the airport in Durban where our hosts awaited to take us to our hotel. We arrived at the beach just north of Umhlanga and stayed on the ninth floor of a beautiful hotel overlooking the ocean.

We got a refreshing sleep and made the one-mile breakfast walk to Zara's Cafe, a wonderful Greek place on the water. Most of the people from the fellowship in Durban were Indian. Durban is home to the largest population of Indians outside of India in the world, about a third of Durban's population of nearly four million. We hung out with a few of these young men on the first day while we overcame our jet lag. That night we had a terrific meal with them and then headed to the room to talk and watch some rugby on TV. I had been reading Brad's first book, and we discussed some of its contents. What quickly became apparent to Brad was that I had become "religious" or "pharisaical" in my belief system. It had been about seven years since I had my encounter with Jesus, and in the meantime I developed a methodical, rules-based, performance-oriented, and humanistic approach to what had now become a troubled walk with the Lord. Given my upbringing in athletics and being a driven businessman regressed by attempting to work or earn my salvation. (Here salvation does not mean 'fire insurance' but rather refers to my journey with the Lord.) Essentially, I had lost my First Love; sadly, the Lord admonished the church at Ephesus for this error. (43)

The Lord told Brad that I was about to be washed by His Holy Spirit, and the Lord's Spirit came in our room that night and moved mightily to correct / help me. This washing was something that occurred the entire eight days that I was in South Africa. The next day upon returning from breakfast we noticed that the safe in our room was flashing red, and upon inspection determined that five hundred dollars had been stolen from my wallet. The following morning when I was paying for breakfast, I discovered that my credit card was stolen as well. There was a prophetic message from the Lord in these acts of thievery that pointed to how satan had stolen things from me, including my very identity. (Jesus said, "The thief does not come except to steal, and to kill, and to destroy. I have come that they may have life, and that they may have it more abundantly.") (44) I called the eight hundred number for Chase and reported the theft of my card. We had about an hour before we were to be picked up for a flight to Pretoria, the capital, so I decided to take a walk on the beach.

CREDIT CARD TRANSLATION

While these seemingly terrible things were happening to me, the Holy Spirit was giving me my life and joy back. Before the flight, I prayed for the Lord to visit me (I mean that literally.) While I walked along this beautiful beach. (45) I recall having so much fun as I watched people surf and swim. A Labrador retriever ran up to me, and when its owner came, I shared the gospel with her and told her that all things were possible with Christ. When she left, I thanked God for giving me my identity back, and I had a thought that if Brad and I would pray together that just maybe the Lord would return my stolen credit card to my wallet. I recalled the mighty evangelist, William Branham, who came to Durban and really flowed in a miracle ministry. Why couldn't God do that for me and Brad? Then I thought, why do I need Brad? So, I prayed the simplest prayer as I shouted, "Grace, Grace!" (46) I then reached into my wallet and pulled out my stolen credit card which obviously, yet significantly, had my name on it. The Lord had translated it supernaturally back to me, and I had my identity back.

On a side note, one of the other crazy things that happened to me while I was there, which was part of this washing of the Lord, happened in every one of the meetings Brad conducted. We had two or more meetings daily, and when the presence of God would come, I would get so emotional and couldn't help myself. This might seem silly but during most of the meetings there the presence of God (Papa) would come so strong that I cried the whole time. I also felt a love and connection to these humble Indian South Africans, so much so, that once I looked at them, I would just bust out sobbing. The Lord was cleansing me from many issues, including a hardness, an improper religious, procedural way of approaching Him, fear, and other things. This trip was a "mountain-top" experience for me.

BACK TO THE BEACH

I looked at my watch and realized I had ten minutes to get back to the room, yet I was on sand and a mile away. When I ran into the room Brad said that it looked like I had seen a ghost and asked me what had happened. I told him the story (which is now in a YouTube video), we got a ride to the airport, and slept on our flight to Pretoria.

Upon arrival at the church we had an enormous, delectable meal, which was always the norm given the kindness of the mostly African Indian community there, and then Brad spoke to a crowd of about three hundred. At the conclusion he called me up front and we shared what had happened to me on the beach. Next, we asked if anyone needed prayer for anything to come forward. They formed two lines behind Brad and me. I had faith for anything after that beach experience. The first person that I prayed for was a teenage girl that fell to the floor, seemingly unconscious, as soon I began to pray. She lay there on the floor for more than an hour and then began to writhe like a snake on the carpet. Brad came over and delivered her of a demon, as he prayed with such care and love that she was eternally changed. Also, significantly, I recall praying for a small child that had AIDS, and I saw His blood flowing through her body in the Spirit realm.

We had some pastoral meetings in Pretoria the next day, and Brad left me behind while he flew back to Durban. I then had a couple of additional meetings with some of the pastors we had met before I was to fly back to the U.S. in two days. But before I left, I had a South African barbecue to attend. This dinner was a miracle in and of itself. Remember I played rugby for the local club about seven years before I became a Christian. A young man from South Africa showed up in our community and joined the team in Shreveport. He had nowhere to live so I invited him to stay at our house. To make a long story very short, he stayed, and I moved out. Years later when he found out that I was going to Pretoria he insisted that I look up his family there. We wound up having an incredible barbecue outside cooked from their brick oven, and we talked about Jesus. Also noteworthy and surreal was that when I went upstairs to use the bathroom I saw a picture of my oldest two daughters on the wall in the hallway! When I departed, they left me with a couple pounds of South African wild game jerky called Biltong. Amusingly, with my newfound freedom I successfully evaded the beagles at customs in Atlanta which were there to catch people like me. Never again!

DEAF MAN AT THE AIRPORT

One of the local senior pastors drove me back to the airport at Jo-burg for my return flight to the states. We ate a wonderful meal, and I cried once more, wondering when I would see these incredible people again. Before boarding the plane, I made one last trip to the rest room. Inside, I couldn't help but notice a powerfully, muscularly built large black man standing by the wall. He had a big rectangular name tag that read, "I am deaf." After I washed my hands, I knew that I was supposed to pray for him. This was a crowded bathroom, and he seemingly could not speak or hear. I looked into these most loving eyes and made a gesture with my hands to pray for him. He smiled and nodded "yes" as I put my hands on his head and shoulders and prayed fervently with all that was in me. I may not have ever felt the Lord's presence as strong as I did there, and it accompanied me all the way to my seat on the airplane. Sitting in my seat reflecting upon what had just happened as I awaited departure, I felt that I heard that I was praying for the Lord's body which is strong and powerful, yet deaf and dumb and needing to be awakened to its true destiny in Christ, the Head. We really need to know Him so that we can hear His voice, do His will, and be a mouthpiece for His kingdom and its purposes.

(Note: Don't miss the hidden mystery in this paragraph.)

I returned to Shreveport changed and with a freedom I had never experienced before. My joy had been restored and I was feeling quite reenergized. At the time we were in home fellowship, the core of which included Mickey, my brother, and Brad's mother, Pat. Our home fellowship met twice monthly. In addition, Stacey and I felt led to worship at The Christian Center of Shreveport as well. Upon my return the pastor there, Timothy, gave me a word of knowledge (47) that confirmed my freedom and identity that had been restored. He said that he saw me in the Spirit pulling people out of a bird cage with my thumb and index finger, and in so doing they were set free from their religious or pharisaical captivity that had previously kept them in bondage. (48)

Since that time, we mostly worshipped in home fellowship which we found to be much more intimate or familial than traditional Sunday worship. We didn't oppose that; however, it was more of an issue of obedience. We also went to several multi-day conferences most years. We believe that conferences have been used in America for very significant impartations of the Lord for the equipping of the saints. (49) Our home fellowships generally consisted of praise and worship, a teaching of whatever the Lord gave whoever from among us gave the message, and prayer for whoever wanted or needed it afterwards. After Jack passed we continued to meet with his wife Pat while she lived in Shreveport, and during these meetings we generally broke bread together with some wonderful home cooking where everyone would bring something tasty.

My friend Mickey and I had attended conferences with so called name brand charismatic / prophetic speakers for years. We have most fond of apostolic ministries based in Fort Mill, South

Carolina, (Rick Joyner / Morning Star Ministries) and another in Redding, California. (Bill Johnson / Bethel Church) For a season we enjoyed hearing cutting edge revelation from an East Indian prophet named Sadhu Sundar Selvaraj and his friend from Australia, Neville Johnson, both of whom typically came to America once annually.

After our friends Brad, wife Susan, and his mother Pat moved to Alabama, and later Myrtle Beach, South Carolina, we started fellowshipping with them twice monthly through video conferencing on our TV set. These meetings are so fresh with revelatory messages straight from heaven. I start each morning in God's word with time to reflect upon His daily bread, my spiritual food to know or attempt to understand what He would have me to do each day, a partnership with His Spirit in my journey with Him. At one time of my life I had a teaching tape in my car most of the time, but that season seems to have ended. Our meetings have focused on equipping us for whatever we need, giving us revelation, wisdom and understanding from above so that we can be a light that goes out into a dark world bringing forth life, the abundant way of the resurrected Jesus who resides within us, with the help of His Holy Spirit whom He sent to be our Co-worker each day. Restated, we are really simply learning how to live life to the fullest extent by denying our own lives, carrying our cross daily, and modeling our savior Jesus (50). In so doing I also look for opportunities each day to share God's love with someone who desperately needs it.

SECOND TRIP
TO SOUTH AFRICA

On Thursday the nineteenth of October 2017, I boarded a plane with my friend Stephen from Myrtle Beach for a twelve-day trip, once again, to see our family in South Africa. As we were descending into Johannesburg on the final approach the flight got exceptionally bumpy and the pilot announced that we had to change our direction down the runway by 180 degrees, to runway 21, or heading 210 degrees. When I heard that my spirit quickened that there was a message from the Lord in our circumstances for the people we were coming to see. I heard Revelation 2:1 and opened my Bible on the descent to a passage I was familiar with that was spoken by Jesus to the church at Ephesus. (51) To paraphrase, He told them some things they were doing right, but that they had "lost their First Love." They needed to make a 180 degree turn and repent. They were encouraged by the first verse in the passage stating that He was walking in their midst and wanted to visit them. I had the opportunity to tell them my story from eight years prior where I regained my identity after it had been stolen from me, along with this message.

Once we landed, I soon discovered that Delta had failed to load my bags in Atlanta, so I had no luggage. After some wonderful fellowship and a good night's rest some of the guys took me to the mall to get some clothing and other things. One of the items I purchased was a rugby jersey of the local pro team, the Durban Sharks, and I wore it right out of the store. While driving from the mall my friend Silvanus recalled that the Sharks had made it to the semifinals of the pro postseason, and since we were close, we should try to get tickets. The game started in about an hour.

The air was full of excitement as we entered the large stadium and parked. We soon found a line to acquire tickets and stood a few minutes until I felt a tap on my shoulder. We all turned to the man who asked us the craziest question, "Would you gentleman like to have complimentary referee passes to the game? I am the chief timekeeper." Why did he pick us out, and who / what was he? I felt the strongest presence of God as the hair on my arms stood straight up and goose bumps emerged; the others felt this manifestation that couldn't be missed. We most joyfully looked at each other astonishingly, with ear to ear smiles, while we said 'yes' in unison. After thoroughly enjoying the Sharks victory over the Pretoria Blue Bulls, we drove home to hang out and converse over some wonderful South African Indian food.

We called and Facebooked our shepherd, Brad, back in the states to share this incredible story. He confirmed this was indeed clearly a message from the Lord. He was granting us more Kingdom authority as evidenced by the referee passes, and the chief timekeeper represented perfect timing on our part. We still don't know if he was an angel or a man! Additionally, we were right where we were supposed to be in the will of the Lord! It mattered not that I still didn't have my luggage for a couple more days. One of the things that I have noticed from my two trips to South Africa...when you make a commitment to go to faraway places (see great commission in Mark 16) in His will, He moves mightily on your behalf, in my case, too indescribable for words.

JESUS WALKING IN THE MIDST OF THE CHURCH, HIS FAMILY

I pray that what I am about to write will ruin some of the readers who hopefully believe and experience this. Something early on that really shook me was hearing some speakers talk at prophetic conferences about time they had spent walking and talking with Jesus on Earth. Ponder that statement again, literally. This is something that I never heard growing up in the mainstream church. When I read the book of Numbers and about the encounters that Moses had with the Lord, and many other people experiencing the Lord in person, I began to yearn, dream, and long for my own experiences with my Maker. The Lord said, "...as for my servant Moses, I speak to him face to face...in the form of a man (Jesus)." (52) We have a better covenant. If Moses could experience God in person, why can't you? I believe that just before God gave Moses the Ten Commandments, He really desired for all to have what Moses had, but because Israel did not want it, they were given

Moses as a mouthpiece for God, and they got the law. Moses even desperately pleaded with Papa that all of Israel were prophets. (53) I have many acquaintances that spend a lot of time focusing on the Lord's return. Without any doubt my perspective is that He has already returned, and I look for Him each day. The Biblical return of Him is accurate, but that is a corporate return for His bride, us, when His church has been perfected and is 'without spot or wrinkle'. (54) The Bible tells that Jesus was seen by more than 500 people after His resurrection. (55) We also read that Jesus was slain before the foundation of the world. (56) That is how Jesus was able to say, "Your father Abraham rejoiced to see My day, and he saw it and was glad." (57) Abraham knew Jesus, as did many other Old Testament prophets like Moses, Isaiah, Jeremiah, David, etc. While Jesus is seated on the throne next to God the Father Almighty (58), He is also omnipresent. He has been walking the earth since before Adam and, from my experience, continues today. Jesus told the seven churches in

Revelation 2 that He walks in their midst, and He is the same yesterday, today, and tomorrow (59).

About five years ago Mickey's son Gabriel had a vision where he saw me stepping out of my house and walking towards the planted shrubs. He then saw me parting the bushes and entering another realm. A month or two after Mickey shared this with me, it actually happened. I have a secret place deep in the forest of what I believe is the most beautiful real estate in Louisiana, in a national forest park. Approximately one hundred miles from my doorstep, the last six miles on dirt roads, far from any humans, I go there to walk, fish, and meditate all day. When I enter the forest, I pray that heaven would manifest on earth, that I would meet the Lord and anybody He wants to bring with Him, and that the creation would come into alignment with His divine purposes. Much of what I have experienced is far too personal to share at this time, yet I write this in the hope that you experience so much more.

THE KISATCHIE
NATIONAL FOREST

During September 2010, Stacey and I went to a multi-day prophetic conference in Fort Mills, South Carolina called Harvest Fest. We were both very excited about seeing Brad, our shepherd, just to hang out and spend some time together, but also because I had been tricked by the enemy and had wandered off the Lord's path for us. This was emotionally both quite painful and embarrassing for Stacey and myself. Essentially, I became overconfident about some important life decisions and completely missed the boat. You would have to be a close, personal friend for me to elaborate on this any further, but essentially, in a nutshell, I framed some things and made decisions wrongly based upon fear and what I perceived to be right or wrong, rather than faith and living life with reckless abandon. Missing God in this season had extreme consequences, so therefore we were miserable and desperate for some new guidance and direction. When we caught up to Brad and visited with him, he tried to help me, but couldn't because I did not have "ears to hear" his response to our situation. However, he did tell me that the Lord was going to visit me in the next month, October. On October 30th nothing had occurred, so I called Brad and reminded him that I was supposed to have a visitation during October, to which he replied with confidence, "Yes, I told you October."

That prompted me to get up at 4 a.m. and drive one hundred miles to the Kisatchie national forest the next morning. As I entered into this beautiful place, I asked the Lord to bring heaven to Earth, to release the animal kingdom into its destiny, and to visit me along with any of the saints that have gone on before us with Him, if He so desired. I proceeded to walk the white sandy bayou about 4 miles north, while taking in His beautiful creation and fishing for Kentucky Spotted Bass.

Upon entering a picturesque rocky, rapid part of the bayou I noticed several men on horseback cross the bayou and head towards me. I had never been able to venture this far north along this stream with my knee-high rubber boots because in certain places the river is impenetrable due to deep holes or fallen trees and high embankments, etc. But this day I may have walked about four miles in one direction, to discover this rocky area with boulders and rapids, and large trees with vines of ripe muscadines shading my path. This setting was so incredibly beautiful that it did indeed feel like heaven on Earth. Also most unusual was that deer hunting season had begun. I wore an orange cap for this reason, even though hunting was not permitted along this gorgeous river. However, to get to where I was the men on horseback would have had to traverse land with hunters, a seemingly most dangerous situation. Two of the men riding, twins, approached me and asked me how to get back to Bethel Cemetery. They noted that I was fishing, asked where I liked to fish, and where I was from. I told them that I often fished on private land in Desoto Parish, Louisiana, the Anderson farm. They both told me that they knew Mrs. Anderson. I responded by stating that Mrs. Anderson had died quite some time ago. This dialogue and backdrop seemed so surreal, like I was in another realm as the twins both nodded to me that they understood she had passed. I then asked if they knew her two daughters that were friends of mine, to which they responded negatively. They then joyfully told me that they were headed back to Bethel Cemetery, smiled and trotted off. Shortly thereafter, another Man came riding up to me on a mule. This was a long straight stretch of this gorgeous white sandy bayou, which again, resembled a shaded tunnel because of the lively, thick canopy covering overhead. I was standing there smoking a cigar and holding my fishing rod in disbelief as this fatherly looking man galloped towards me with purpose and confidence...to converse with ME. Our most intimate dialogue confirmed Brad's

October visitation, but is much too personal to share. I walked the three or so miles south on the bayou with my head in the clouds pondering every millisecond of this experience over and over and over…, then drove home wrecked with joy, again, thinking and dreaming through every moment of the visitation during the two-hour drive back.

Interestingly, I had lunch with one of the Anderson daughters the following week and she professed to me that she had embraced a universalistic message or belief system espoused by her pastor at the local Methodist church, just like her deceased mom had. But I knew differently, I told her, as I then shared that the two twins knew her mom, and she couldn't be a Universalist because there exists only one path to God, the path her mom followed, and that is through His Son, the risen Lord Jesus! The twins that I met were part of the "great cloud of witnesses" who often accompany Jesus during His endeavors on Earth. (60) The giveaway to this parabolic adventure for me was that there was no Bethel Cemetery on the map. Bethel, in the Bible, was where Jacob laid his head to rest on a rock and had visions of angels ascending and descending a ladder, back and forth from heaven, where the Lord stood above the ladder. (61) Stating that they were from Bethel Cemetery was an admission that they were deceased yet alive forevermore and part of "the cloud." So again, clearly, the name "Bethel" represented a gateway or ladder for saints who have passed from this realm to the next.

Just before Jesus hung on the cross He was interrogated by Caiaphas, the high priest. When asked if He was the Christ, the Son of God, He replied in the affirmative, then stated…."hereafter you will see the Son of Man sitting at the right hand of the Power and coming on the clouds of heaven." Herein lies the most wonderful message that while Christ is seated on the throne at the right hand of the Father, He is also omnipresent, walking planet Earth with His companions, His beloved saints that have passed before us. (Matthew 26:64)

THE ROAD TO EMMAUS

The Bible states that we may entertain angels unaware (62), and that the Lord Jesus will manifest and reveal Himself to those who keep His commandments and love Him. (63) Two of the Lord's disciples were walking with Him on the road to Emmaus (64) and did not recognize Him until He broke bread with them and opened their eyes. I believe that He is walking the earth everyday just looking for somebody who is so earnestly looking for Him. But just like the two on the road to Emmaus, He comes in many different forms, and we may not recognize Him. When the disciples recognized Him, He immediately vanished (He is sneaky!), and they said, "Did not our heart burn within us while He talked with us on the road, and while He opened the Scriptures to us?" (65)

One morning several years ago I was driving to work on the Clyde Fant Parkway which parallels the Red River in Shreveport. When about a mile from downtown, I looked over to my right along the river and saw an older man riding a bicycle on the bike path. Immediately I felt that burning sensation in my heart. I drove fast to the end of the bike path, parked my car and ran out to the path to meet...the Lord. I stood on the bike path and waited for the man to arrive, and he looked at me like I was nuts when I stopped him and asked him his name. The side of his face sagged from having had a stroke, and he appeared to be about sixty-five years old. After we conversed for a while I jumped into my SUV and drove the rest of the way to work wondering if I had just missed it. I called Brad and he explained that I had actually seen the Lord in another person, like we read about in Matthew 25. "Then the King will say to those on His right hand, 'Come, you blessed of My Father, inherit the kingdom prepared for you from the foundation of the world; 'for I was hungry and you gave Me food; I was thirsty and you gave Me drink; I was a stranger and you took Me in; 'I was naked and you clothed Me; I was sick and you visited Me; I was in prison and you came to Me.' "Then the righteous will answer Him, saying, 'Lord, when did we see You hungry and feed You, or thirsty and give You drink? 'When did we see you a stranger and take You in, or naked and clothe You? 'Or when did we see You sick, or in prison, and come to You?' "And the King will answer and say to them, 'Assuredly, I say to you, inasmuch as you did it to one of the least of these My brethren, you did it to Me." (66) Sometime later we had a yard sale and this man showed up! We wound up talking, visiting, and praying together, and ultimately became friends. God is so good! ... So as already stated I believe that He is walking the earth every day, and on this occasion, I encountered Him through another man.

The greatest, most exciting story ever told is Christ, and you and I have a wonderful opportunity to be a part of this story / testimony that has no end. I live for that EVERY day, to see Him face to face, to encounter Him in the highways and byways! This awakening in me had been waiting, tarrying ever since I was a little boy when I had dreams of literally flying in His presence. I am fully persuaded that the Best is yet to come, my wildest visions of knowing Him are within my grasp in the days ahead!

OUR MOVE TO CRESWELL AVENUE

Our family had lived in a house in South Shreveport near the LSUS campus for twelve years. With some help from Jack McClendon and our in-laws, we did some extensive remodeling over a multi-year period so that we could sell our house and move to a more desirable location to us, preferably even farther south in Shreveport. So, we put our house on the market and almost nothing happened for a period of about 100 days. Then one night, Stacey had a dream in which the

Lord gave her the selling price which was exactly five thousand dollars less than what we had previously been asking. While our real estate agent told us that we would sell the house at the original price, we wanted to be faithful to the Lord, so we reduced the price the next day. Sure enough, two days later we had a contract on the house for the price that we were given in the dream. When we went to the closing, we shared the testimony of Stacey's dream to all who were present and talked about God's goodness. The buyers who were also believers, needed to have the price dropped by the amount given to us or they would have never been able to make the purchase.

We had about six weeks before closing to find a place to live so after looking at a number of newly constructed houses far south of town we decided to make an offer on one that we liked that backed up against a beautiful lake. We drove to the real estate office on a Saturday morning ready to sign the offer. While we were sitting there, literally pen in hand about to sign, I heard my cell phone beep with a text message that came from our friend Brad McClendon. I read the message, "There is something for you in Isaiah 55." We asked the realtor if he had a Bible anywhere and he did not. I keep a pocket Bible in the console of my SUV, but we were in Stacey's Volvo, which upon inspection did not have one. So, we went back inside and I sat there for a couple of minutes with my eyes closed and the Holy Spirit gave me recall of the part I needed to remember from Isaiah chapter 55, specifically verses eight and nine. "For My thoughts are not your thoughts, nor are your ways My ways," says the Lord, "For as the heavens are higher than the earth, so are My ways higher than your ways, and My thoughts than your thoughts."

Immediately I knew that the Lord had better plans for us, and we were not supposed to get this house. This was a tough pill to swallow, especially for Stacey, but I shared the Scripture with the realtor and told him that we couldn't sign anything.

We went home feeling bittersweet; we love so much to hear from God like that, but we now had very little time to move out of our house. With more looking at nothing that felt right we got especially frustrated, and this culminated in Stacey and me praying on a Friday morning before I left for work, having to be moved within a week. We held hands and prayed a prayer of desperation. I got in my car and headed to work. Stacey called about five minutes later and said that there was another house for sale or rent that she discovered in that morning's Shreveport Times with a cell phone number which I immediately phoned. The builder answered and asked if I could turn around and meet him at the house which was less than a mile from where we were living. I met Harry there, looked at the house, and asked that he hold onto it until we both could get a thorough look that afternoon. We came back and spent about two hours with him. Stacey liked this large new house, but it wasn't quite the home that we envisioned so we ultimately worked out a rental agreement.

What was really interesting about the builder was how he had health issues that greatly saddened us. Specifically, he had heart problems with a heart ejection fraction of about 15 on a scale of one to one hundred. His doctors had told him that he was the walking dead; it was surprising to them that he could even walk around each day without falling out. So, we quickly looked at the house with him, and listened to him regarding his health issues. We knew that we were meant to pray for him, so I started sharing some healing testimonies with him, and how Jesus came to heal every sickness and disease. We laid hands on his chest and prayed and prayed. About a week later Harry came by the house on a rainy Sunday afternoon, knocked on our door, and then declared how Jesus healed his heart. The doctors were confounded how his heart ejection fraction went from 15 to over 60, terrific for a man over 70 years of age.

We were thrilled about Harry's new lease on life, as well as his testimony. But we had intended to stay in this house, which was not ideal, for only about six months. Six months went by and we were still renting until 37 months elapsed. Then one day we were riding bicycles in town and rode by a house on Creswell Avenue. This was a beautiful 90-year-old house that a builder had completely restored. There was a "For Sale" sign in the front yard, and Stacey asked if I would call the number so we could take a look. We learned that the sign had only been there a few days. Upon inspection this felt perfect to us and was central to all of Shreveport. The house had a large yard for the dogs, among other amenities, and the front gate had a large "D" on it. When I saw that, I knew it was the Lord. We purchased Stacey's dream house, and we are still here!

MEMORABLE ENCOUNTERS WITH NATURE

THE GREAT BLUE HERON

When I graduated from high school, my paternal grandparents invited me to visit them at the Florida gulf coast. While they were believers, I was not at the time. One day they took me to the coast to fish with live shrimp for speckled trout. I was standing on the bank near a bridge fishing when I saw a Great Blue Heron way off in the distance begin to fly towards me. This enormous graceful bird was on a path approaching me, and I thought that he would fly directly over my head, when suddenly, he flew right at me and landed at my feet. He had such long legs that his head came up to my chest, and his beak was about six inches long. In the wild these creatures are very shy and most often fly before you can get very close to them. When he landed, an anointing from heaven touched my body and made my hair stand straight up. I then fed him all of my remaining shrimp; he hung out with me for a little while; and then took off flying again. As I write this, I recall John 3:16 because the Lord is so gracious to the just and the unjust, like me, unjust at that time. "For God so loved the world," lost people like me, that while I was so far from Him and still a lost sinner, He did this for me. Because I have a love for His creation which He put in me before the foundation of the world, He was showing me in my late teenage years something that I would not understand for decades, a calling to work alongside the animal kingdom harmoniously and purposefully, with God, as Paul wrote, (67) in order to come into the alignment of heaven and the divine purposes that He has for us in the coming days.

Herons are quite common where we live now in Louisiana, and I believe the Lord has put them in my path to give me a message of standing firm in Him...and being patient. There was a season while driving to work that I would frequently see one motionless on the side of the parkway that paralleled the Red River. One day I stood out in our back yard and asked the Lord to release His creation into its destiny within our midst where we live. While having read about this in the Bible, I really don't understand much about what this means, nor what is coming in the future, aside from recently grasping that nature and the animal kingdom help us to understand God's times and seasons, or what He is about to do in the Earth. Interestingly, we had a goldfish pond with about 15 or so fish in our back yard, not twenty feet from the house. The next day I came home from work and saw a heron standing in the pond. My daughters began to cry because they obviously liked the goldfish. So, I ran outside and made him fly away, walked back into the house to calm down the kids, and when I later trudged outside to survey the damage, he was standing on the rooftop of the house watching me. The next morning, I recall also that most unusually, a group of Canada geese flew over our house making an extraordinary amount of racket while flying only about ten feet over our heads. I believe that they were speaking in a tongue that one day in the future, hopefully, we may understand.

On several occasions I walked up to Red-tailed and Cooper's hawks in my back yard. I got no more than five feet away from these birds while talking to them; again, I felt the presence of the Lord, and the birds stayed put and looked at me as if they were awaiting instruction. I had a similar experience mid-afternoon riding my bike in the country when I encountered a huge Barred owl, a creature that is normally nocturnal. I got off my bike, walked about 15 feet from him and waited for a message from God, which came forth parabolically through his actions the next few minutes. Essentially, the message was that in order for me to fly higher and see with real vision and wisdom, I needed to be fearless and wait on God, patiently resting in Him. While in the Louisiana Kisatchie National forest, I walked up to a wild coyote and tossed some crackers to him. Another morning as I was leaving the house to go to work, I noticed an Olive Warbler standing at the back door, apparently waiting for me. I opened the door and knelt down only a foot away from him. Again, he looked like he wanted instruction from me before he flew off, or perhaps he had a message for me, yet I was not yet spiritually mature enough to get it. As I have already previously mentioned the Lord has sent white doves to us, I believe to show us that He is with us, watching us, looking out for us.

My wife and I have been to Costa Rica a number of times and we have had most unusual experiences with Scarlet Macaws and Toucans which have at times put on a show for us. These birds are extremely rare to see in the wild, yet we see them regularly when we go there. Now when we travel there, we pray for Him, with great expectation, to show us His animal kingdom. I believe that the Lord really appreciates our love for His creation.

THE HUMMINGBIRD IN COSTA RICA

Several years ago, Stacey and I were vacationing In Costa Rica. Every morning we were awakened by parrots and parakeets at about 5:30. So I typically made coffee and went outside to read and take in the wildlife. One morning while reading I heard a thump sound and noticed a hummingbird had flown into the window, fell, and appeared dead. I picked him up, cupped him in my hands and prayed like the house was on fire. When I opened my hands, he came to and flew away. About six months later we were at the same place in Costa Rica. I was sitting in the rocker, reading again early in the morning when, apparently, the same hummingbird flew about eighteen inches from my face and hovered for about thirty seconds there. I again felt the presence of God as I knew that he was thanking me for having prayed for him six months prior. There was a real tangible, literal communication, yet no words were spoken.

FISHING TRIP WITH
MY SPIRITUAL FATHER
(ANOTHER JACK MCCLENDON STORY)

Sometime in the spring of 2007 I was invited to go fishing with my mentor, Jack McClendon. We went to a lake in southern Arkansas on an unusually chilly Saturday. A cold front had just come through which ruined the fishing, so it was one of the few, perhaps the only time that we did not catch a single fish. We saw some large alligators, and did have a few nibbles, but about midday we decided to try an area near the bridge where we parked before returning home. Suddenly there were some birds carrying on near the bank in some tall pine trees. The Holy Spirit came into the boat in a powerful way, and Jack and I wondered greatly what was about to happen next. A huge bald eagle flew out of the tree and soared in the sky until we left. About five seconds after he flew out, the largest woodpecker I have ever seen flew out of the same tree. This may seem hard to grasp, but the woodpecker was a long documented extinct

Ivory-Billed Woodpecker, which was significantly larger than a crow, about twenty inches in length with a thirty-inch wingspan. There is a very similar Pileated woodpecker, fully a third smaller, with less white on the upper part of the wing, among other differences. Upon both of us seeing this bird, I told Jack to take a good look so that we could confirm that it was indeed the extinct variety. Immediately upon my return to the house I got out my bird books to confirm what we had witnessed.

I had previously read an article that was published by Cornell ornithologists on April 28th of 2005, regarding a supposed sighting in Arkansas during the prior year. I remember this because the 28th just so happens, significantly, to be my birthday, and I felt that the Lord used this as a message to me. This communication was confirmed by what Jack and I saw in Arkansas that day. I believe that in most spiritual encounters with God of any kind, there is a profound mystery for us to seek out. In this case, the eagle represented Jack and the woodpecker revealed something missing from the body of Christ for a long time, specifically, the ministry of deliverance. The Ivory-Billed woodpecker was called the Lord God bird by the Indians long ago because the birds had a cry that sounded like, "Lord God, Lord God." The bill, which is long and ivory colored, is used to make large holes in dead trees about the size of a quarter or half dollar. Trees, like the Tree of Life (Jesus) in the Bible are often symbolic of people. So, the extinct woodpecker prophetically spoke of deliverance ministries from long ago that were now largely extinct from church ministry. The last confirmed sightings of the Ivory-Billed woodpecker were in the mid-1940s, a time when we had William Branham and Derrick Prince from Indiana and the U.K., both of whom had flourishing deliverance ministries, a ministry about setting the captives free from addiction, demonic activities, bondage, mental disorders, and other problems.

I actually called the ornithologists at Cornell to discover that they had given up on seeing these birds and didn't really care to speak with me. I have seen this bird on at least one other occasion in a Louisiana National forest.

BARKLEY

Stacey's all-time favorite pet was a dog, Barkley, we got for Christmas about 25 years ago. He was trained to do quite a few things for us such as getting the newspaper every morning, and he really seemed to walk in unconditional love. At twelve years of age he developed cancerous tumors and our vet advised us to put him down. Incredibly, though in terrible shape, he never complained. We had him put to sleep and I buried him on a farm in Desoto Parish. Shortly thereafter Stacey was standing in the kitchen and looked outside the backdoor to see Barkley standing there looking in through the glass in the door. The Lord allowed him to come show us that he was in another realm and we will one day be united with him once again.

Stacey and I have observed a fully lucent (albino) migratory red-tailed hawk that comes to Shreveport every November for the past five or so years. Once I asked the Lord for a sign that I had been praying about and His answer came in another sighting and picture that I took of this brilliant white hawk. On the photograph you can see a halo of the Lord over this bird, with the accompanying meaning that He is always with me. We believe that as the body of Christ comes into the fullness of the Lord's "restoration of all things," that we will see him use nature and wildlife to help His body better understand the times and seasons of our Lord's plans. Our hearts burn to be a part of this awakening of our communion with Him, His body, and His creation.

OUR BLUE TICK HEELER HOUND NAMED JOHN

Our friend Brad was staying with us not long ago and eating breakfast alongside our two male beggars, John the hound, and Buddy, our black lab. John had been lying there on the kitchen floor somewhat patiently until he couldn't stand it anymore, so he asked Brad for a bite...in the Spirit. Brad excitedly shouted to me that he had heard John in the Spirit asking him for a bite of his breakfast. Loud! So, for the next six months I prayed without ceasing wanting to know for myself that we might be able to communicate with the animal kingdom nonverbally (just like most or all heavenly communication). I wanted to hear John. Then one morning I was making, I have to say, an amazing breakfast that took thirty minutes or so, with John again seemingly patiently waiting. When I was nearly done eating, I gave him a bite of my omelet and unmistakably got rocked by him thanking me in the Spirit, "Thank you, Jack." This was so loud, it turned me; it seemed so close to being audible. John's voice booms in the natural as well, especially when he knows he is going for a ride in Stacey's Volvo.

After this morning, our relationship changed noticeably. John had been abused before we rescued him, but he knew that I had heard him, was also a heavenly creature, and now there was an increase in trust. I don't care what anyone, Bible scholar or teacher, says about whether animals have a spirit or not because I now know by experience. I haven't yet heard John's older brother, Buddy, but I'm convinced that's just because I haven't been sensitive to his language, and one day I will. To take this experience a little further...I'm fully persuaded that every blade of grass, mosquito, tree, and animal all have a Spirit that God placed in them, and when they pass from this realm to the next, our Lord is there waiting for them with open arms and a love that, for us, takes a lifetime to comprehend...only partially.

JORDAN CROSSING 318

During April 2017, I was reading my Bible early in the morning when I couldn't help but notice that water droplets appeared on the passage I was engaging, the beginning of Acts, Chapter 13. I wondered if my eyes or nose had dripped as I wiped the water off the page and smeared some of the ink where I have marked these pages. This happened three times, just enough for me to wake up to the realization that Papa wanted to say something to me.

"Now in the church that was at Antioch there were certain prophets and teachers: Barnabas, Simeon who was called Niger, Lucius of Cyrene, Manaen who had been brought up with Herod the tetrarch, and Saul. As they ministered to the Lord and fasted, the Holy Spirit said, 'Now separate to Me Barnabas and Saul for the work to which I have called them.' Then, having fasted and prayed, and laid hands on them, they sent them away."

Recall that we had been in home fellowship with Jack and Pat McClendon beginning in early 2004. Jack passed on St. Patty's Day, 2008, and while Brad was directing the funeral in southern Arkansas, we all heard the horn of a train passing by, yet there were no trains or tracks for miles. The train represented the Lord's plans for a move of God in Shreveport which Jack was faithful to initiate. So, with his passing, father Jack handed the conductor's baton to son Brad who, at the time, visited us in Shreveport several times annually. Additionally, we began Skyping together with Brad during 2013. During one of his visits he Skyped with a number of churches in Nova Scotia from our home. I sat through the meeting and asked if he would feed, do the same, with some hungry people we knew, mostly the ones he visited here. So, we began to Skype twice monthly from our home in the evenings, wonderfully anointed meetings, which we are still doing. Sometime during 2017 Brad came to Shreveport to see us all, but also to officiate the marriage of his brother

Todd and fiancé Holly. This celebration was held at my business partner and longtime close, personal friend, Bill's house, outdoors on their wooden deck. During the middle of this ceremony, we were again interrupted by the horn of a loud train coming down the nearby tracks.

When I was so moved by the water droplets bubbling up in my Bible, I called Brad, and he told me that it was time for our group to take on its own identity. As the passage indicated, in a sense we needed to "separate ourselves" from Brad and become our own family with our own messages. He would continue to Father us, but it was time to step out and conduct our meetings and teachings and press forward in developing and culturing the relationships that had been unfolding. We continued to Skype once per month, and started Wednesday night meetings, moving from home to home until June of 2018 when Brad told us that we needed to take another step towards looking more like a church, but not to pattern this based upon any kind of reasoning, tradition, or human logic. We wanted to hear from heaven.

The Lord had been getting Brad's attention from his home in Myrtle Beach. Initially, when it was impressed upon him that he was going to be spending a lot more time in Shreveport and potentially moving here, he didn't like the idea of being uprooted again. So, he told the Lord that if He gave us a building (without telling us), he would move here. So, my colleague, Bill, and I began talking to some folks that we were connected to about renting a building. Then Bill, brother David, and I went to look at several places that we could potentially use and rent. One of the buildings was mentioned to Bill, in passing, while he was visiting an acquaintance named Gary. The last place we visited that day was Gary's and when we walked around in the space the anointing came heavily and brought understanding that, without a doubt, this was the place. Shocking to us, he offered it to us for free until January 2019.

In early 2018 we were all praying for a name for our church family when a few of us, initially my wife, Stacey, heard Jordan Crossing. Bill did all the paperwork to file with the Secretary of State, but our name had been taken, so we added our area code to the new name, Jordan Crossing 318. The paperwork was filed on a Friday in March of 2018, or 3:18. The next day Jesse Stokely (remember Christian Alliance in Houston) visited our fellowship and gifted us a stock certificate worth $30,000 during a Saturday meeting that Brad directed in our home. The timing of this is stunning; it was a Biblical first fruits offering given on the first day possible that we had a name, which was needed on the stock certificate.

We also received several Scriptures to confirm our identity and name. 1 John 3:18, My little children, let us not love in word or in tongue, but in deed and in truth.

Deuteronomy 31:8, And the LORD, He is the one One who goes before you. He will be with you. He will not leave you nor forsake you; do not fear nor be dismayed.

2 Corinthians 3:18, But we all, with unveiled face, beholding as in a mirror the glory of the Lord, are being transformed into the same image from glory to glory, just as by the Spirit of the Lord.

John 3:18, He who believes in Him is not condemned; but he who does not believe is condemned already, because he has not believed in the name of the only begotten Son of God.

In Genesis 14, Abraham's family army of 318 successfully warred and defeated those who had captured his nephew Lot. Our friend Brad and a witness, his friend Larry, were given a prophetic Word that this passage (and area code 318) was for our church family here in Shreveport.

Joshua 3:18. Most significant to me personally, Joshua 3 ends with verse 17 where Israel walks across the Jordan River on dry ground to enter the Promised Land. Jordan Crossing 318 is part of that Joshua generation, 3:18, the yet unwritten and unenacted part of the Jordan Crossing that facilitates the great harvest at the end of the Age to come, to hasten the Lord's return for a bride that is without spot or wrinkle. (68) Our friends Brad and Susan are now committed and planning their move to Shreveport to shepherd our church family.

PAT MCCLENDON MOVES BACK TO SHREVEPORT

I have recently added this story to the narrative because it contains something spectacularly supernatural that displays God's awesome power and goodness. Brad's mother Pat felt like she had clearly heard from the Lord that she was supposed to follow her son on this new venture to Shreveport once she was able to sell her house in Myrtle

Beach. This occurred fairly quickly, and she soon found a home that seemed right for her in Louisiana. While Brad was speaking at JC318 during July 2019 I felt like I heard that I was supposed to fly to Myrtle and help Pat move here.

On August 1, I flew to Myrtle Beach so that we could make the 960-mile trek the following day. As I walked through the Atlanta airport, I realized that I had forgotten one of my baseball caps that I generally like to wear when I'm not in the office. So, I strolled into a gift shop and purchased a blue hat that had Atlanta, GA prominently displayed. We awakened early to make the long drive the following day. Brad was driving a 26-foot U-Haul truck with a trailer attached, and I drove Pat's car with her seated next to me. We initially planned to take two days for this excursion.

We had been grinding away on the Interstate highway for some time as we began to enter Atlanta. It takes about an hour to make it across this large city which had horrific traffic. We had driven about ten minutes after I noticed more traffic and the widening of the Interstate before I got a phone call from Brad whom I was following. When I answered my cell, the Holy Spirit whacked me and Pat in the car before Brad uttered a single word. I had goose bumps and the hair on my arms was standing straight up when he told me to look in the rear-view mirror. Upon inspection, I could see all of the tall buildings in Atlanta behind us, as we were now exiting the outskirts of this large city. What had happened is that the Lord decided to translate us through this difficult part so that we didn't have to sweat it out. He translated us maybe 40 or 50 miles in an instant! When I pondered this, I wondered if perhaps we had been destined for a catastrophic wreck, but when I asked Brad, upon reflection he felt that the Lord had done this, just to show us His goodness and help us out. He gave us another lifetime marker, also to show us that we were on His path, at the right time and season. This also confirmed to Pat that she had chosen the correct course of action or faith in making this move.

With the Lord's help we decided that we could make it the whole way in one day, yet it was still a dawn to dusk trek, with us arriving at my house at about 8:30 that evening. I felt ecstatic that the Lord did this for us. Also crazy is that I believe He ordered my steps in Atlanta in order to purchase my blue baseball cap that is now a memento of a spectacular marker in my lifetime. Blue is God's color for revelation or heaven.

Two Mondays later I was riding my early morning 20-mile ride on my mountain bike before work. My colleague and I had been meeting at 8 a.m. to strategize the coming work week. As I looked at my watch and came to a fork in the road, I contemplated which way I should go so that I wouldn't be late for my meeting. The next thing I notice is that the Lord translated me about 200 meters past the fork to help me make the correct decision. This, again, was mind blowing to me as I praised God during the rest of my ride home. Until now, partly because this is difficult for most to believe, I have not shared this revelation with anybody except Brad. Brad told me that our translation through Atlanta had opened a spiritual door for us to engage in this in the future. If you believe it, you can have it! Interestingly, I recall a dream that I had perhaps ten years ago that foretold these translations. I was talking to some people about Jesus at a train station in Dublin, Ireland. My enthusiasm was so great that a gentleman pointed out to me that I missed the train. I then laughed, told him that it was ok, and I was immediately translated to somewhere else in Ireland that we were traveling to. By the way, this concept of translation is Biblical.

In Acts 8:26-40, Philip shares the Gospel of Jesus with an Ethiopian eunuch who is reading from the book of Isaiah. After Philip gives him understanding, he then baptizes the eunuch before he was "suddenly taken away by the Spirit of the Lord" to Azotus, about 30 miles away, while the Ethiopian "went on his way rejoicing."

While this writing so far may read something like a memoir, that is not at all the case from my perspective; I still feel like I am just getting started in my quest to know God, ecstatic like a small child with a new adventure on the horizon. Isn't He so good!?

PART III

WHAT WAS GOD TEACHING ME THROUGH MY ENCOUNTER?

Warning: Once you get a few pages into Part III you will find that some of this section soon shifts and reads more like a Bible teaching than a story. Some readers will likely find this section interesting and some, not so much. I've added this part because it adds to the story of my life and relates it to God's long-term plans for me and all of His kids. This rendering has also been a great challenge for me as I have never seen this forthcoming analogy written anywhere. In a nutshell, I am linking my encounter and life to the Lord's celebratory feasts in the Old Testament. Should you choose to skip this part, in the final appendix I write about every manner I can recall in which the Lord has communicated with me...our very special and unique love language.

RECOGNITION OF GOD'S HAND IN MY LIFE AFFAIRS

One of the earliest memories that I have of when I was a little boy was an infatuation with a small book I found at my maternal grandparents house. The book had pen and ink drawings (still remembered) of cave men with commentary that went with the artwork. Every time I would visit, I would go straight to that book on the shelf in the den and spend hours completely fascinated by what I saw. It was long after I was born again that I finally understood that Papa had placed a tremendous hunger in me, not just to know Him, but also the origin of man, His family. What an invitation! I am fully persuaded, provided I do my part in this relationship, that one day my Friend will tell me and show me things that perhaps nobody currently fully comprehends. I really do believe a mystery that deep is available to me, of all people, even *moi*.

I can also recall when flying B-52 bombing missions, that whenever we encountered precarious situations, I would have a comfort come over me and the feeling and inner knowledge that I was a survivor. An example of this was when we practiced takeoffs with quite a few bombers yet had only twelve second spacing between each other. We trained these launches during the Cold War with Russia, and the intent was to get all of the nuclear capable aircraft airborne quickly because, under the possibility of certain apocalyptic scenarios, there were likely inbound Soviet nuclear inter-continental ballistic missiles (ICBMs). To further dramatize this, imagine nothing but black exhaust smoke in front of you and powerful turbulence having been created by the air rush wake from the forward, now retired, G-model aircraft. On one occasion during takeoff we got into ninety degrees of bank--that's completely sideways, with virtually no visibility and planes both twelve seconds in front and behind us. The Lord made it clear to me, through peace, a deeply rooted knowledge or understanding, that I was made to endure all such situations in this life; it did not matter whether I bailed out in Moscow or Siberia during February.

WANTING TO KNOW
THE TRUTH

Shortly after I became born again, the fire of God's Spirit residing and resonating in me had so changed me, created within such a deep-seated passion, and made me question the traditional life of the believer in so many ways. I especially wanted to KNOW the Truth about everything that we did in worship and church teaching settings, making decisions about life events, basically how to live the abundant life that I read that Jesus came to bring us. This inspiration made me question everything about God that any man had ever told me to do. I've since learned that the Lord placed in me, even before I was in my mother's womb, a redemptive gift (69) to understand and stand for the Truth, to be a loving confrontationist for Jesus, to blaze trails He set before me with even reckless abandonment, and to lead the way for others. This barometer has seemingly burned in every cell of my body. When the Scriptures came alive to me, I realized that the Gospels and the book of Acts were a history (His Story) about the life of the early church and the acts of the Holy Spirit through the believers during the first century (Acts). I quickly understood that what I had called "Church" did not look like anything that I read about in the Bible...so I wanted to know the origin and why we, for example, celebrated Christmas (on the wrong day), Easter and Lent (neither in the Bible), deviated from God's calendar that is in the Bible, and many other things. Upon discovering the answers to these questions, in some cases I felt that I had and have to go along with some of these traditions, in order to "be all things to all men," yet some things really seemed to suffocate me. I had also already made a decision to fear God and not man. With my focus on Him I began to attempt to discern whether God was in the things that I practiced, and even if not totally, that I had my heart in the right place, and was not critical.

Until I was born again at age forty, I cared little about any of these matters. One of my first observances and questions: having been raised Methodist, was this something that I wanted to conform to?; why were there so many denominations where I lived? (and everywhere else); and why did they practice what they practiced? In the end I learned that I did not want to conform to a group of men in order to be a good Methodist, Catholic, Protestant, good whatever, but rather a child or a son of my Father in heaven. I wanted my life to be a living epistle or continuation of the lives of the believers that I had read about in Acts, the only book in the Bible that does not end in "Amen." I struggled with things like, why did they print a bulletin for the service?; why do they always sing three songs?; why was there a message prepared in advance?; why did we follow the clock with some theatrical presentation?

Where was the guidance of the Holy Spirit? Any serious questions I had, I found were usually countered with responses that made little sense to me or generally opposed, most importantly, my biblical world view. During this time, the Spirit was so strong with me, that I trusted that God would show me where He wanted me to grow in Him.

My point with all of this in hindsight was about discernment, a decade or more of walking out an understanding of the mixture of the church, that is, the part that was God or Spirit, and the part that was humanism. And while still a work in progress, this spiritual awareness came only from knowing The Truth. There was a season in my life where I became critical of any gathering or assembly of God's people that didn't look like what I thought was most correct. This terribly divisive mindset has evolved to where I now most earnestly believe that we desperately need each other, and I certainly do include myself in this imperfect "mixture." We all have different doctrines and when we hear something that is incorrect, I've learned, just "spit the bones out and keep the good meat." The Holy Spirit has been my teacher, and He knows how to get through to us, no matter who gives the message, provided we are open and have hearts to receive God's part or the "Spirit behind the letter."

SPIRITUAL ISRAEL'S "MANDATORY FEASTS" OF THE LORD

During the weekend of August 8th, 2008 (8-8-8), my friend Mickey and I couldn't wait to travel to Baton Rouge for a prophetic conference which featured Australian Neville Johnson and Indian Sadhu Sundar Selvaraj who travelled to the States generally once annually to share revelatory messages. This meeting was cutting edge. Most of the content I had never heard before. The number eight in the Bible often represents a new beginning so this message was meant to be fresh for the body of Christ to move forward, and the date,

8-8-8, was clearly intentional. The focus of their talks was on what was referred to as the mandatory (70) feasts of the Lord: Passover, Pentecost, and Tabernacles, and more importantly, who they point to (Jesus!). Something burned within me to understand more thoroughly why the Lord had Israel keep these feasts until Christ, and why and when most of the church ceased these celebratory practices. It was through this study that the entire Bible opened up and made sense to me, but I was also able to much better understand my encounter, God's purpose for my life, and His inheritance that awaits me (and anybody else who wants all of God). God had Israel practice these feasts in perpetuity for the very simple yet most significant reason: to reveal His Son and thus Himself to all mankind. This personal revelation of the feasts has evolved from a comprehension of biblical church life to just plain life or learning and yearning to know fully how to walk and run abundantly with such joy that we are not moved by anything, attracting others to our peaceful, joyful disposition and countenance...without trying, just living...that, I believe, is what Jesus came to teach us.

EXODUS 12

A few years ago, my family was seated at the dining room table for an Easter lunch when I asked my kids (They are actually in their 20s.) a trick question. When was the first Easter celebration? My answer came from Exodus 12 which is the passage where the Lord commanded Moses to have the Israelites paint both doorposts and the lintel with blood from a lamb that the head of each household sacrificed. That night the family roasted the lamb in the fire and ate it in haste, the entire lamb, including its entrails, with their belts and sandals on, ready to depart Egypt in a hurry. The death angel "passed over" every house which had been obedient to the will of God, but for those who were not, the first born of the family perished (including livestock). Extra-biblical accounts which have been passed down by rabbinical priests for

3,500 years indicate that only a remnant of ten to twenty percent of the Israelites (also some foreigners who had wholeheartedly adopted the Israelites lifestyle and God's commands for them) actually participated in the exodus from Egypt and hastily headed for the Promised Land. The remainder ultimately died out in Egypt. This was the church's first Passover which Israel (whether they understood this or not) celebrated for the next 1500 years until the Real Lamb of God was crucified and resurrected.

So for any Jew, Muslim, Gentile, or whomever contemplates Exodus 12, they see that this story, what God actually made Israel walk out, is prophetic and Holy, because it points to Jesus and the salvation that He brings to the lost of this world. Understand that when I mention Passover that I am actually referring to the feasts of Passover, Unleavened Bread and First Fruits as one, as they all occur during the eight days of The Feast of Unleavened Bread (also broadly referred to as Passover). Technically, our Easter celebration is really, or should be called, First Fruits. Amazingly, Jesus was resurrected on the day of First Fruits. Biblically, He is referred to, among a near infinite number of other names and titles, as the First-Borne of all creation and the First-Fruits of many brethren. (71)

PASSOVER AND EASTER

Most sincere Christians celebrate Easter to commemorate the day that Jesus was resurrected from the dead. However, the first century church which was nearly completely Jewish, celebrated Passover (and Unleavened Bread and First Fruits). It was mandatory for Jews to make a pilgrimage to Jerusalem every Passover until Messiah came. So, Passover was celebrated until Christ as a celebration of God's deliverance from Egypt. But the complete meaning of Passover was revealed to the early Christian Jews when Christ died on the cross. They understood that Passover pointed to a coming out of Egypt or darkness and into the Light

(Jesus), or having been born again. Unleavened bread was eaten to point to Messiah, or Yeshua, cleansing us or making us unleavened from sin. First Fruits then concluded Passover with a celebration and thanksgiving for produce (barley harvest), and later the resurrection of the first First-Fruit (Jesus), and our resurrection as new First-Fruit beings. Jesus said, "I am the Resurrection." (72) The celebration of these feasts by early, mostly Jewish Christians soon, however, came to an end.

Unfortunately, the Romans made a God out of Caesar, required the annual worship of him, destroyed the Jewish Temple in 70 A.D., and began to persecute the Jews. Christianity was legalized in 313 A.D, yet it became unlawful for any Jew or Christian to celebrate Passover after the Nicean Council of 325 A.D. To do so was punishable by death. Passover which is celebrated in accordance with the Jewish calendar was replaced with a celebration called Easter and in accordance with the Roman calendar. The name Easter was derived from the fertility goddess, Ishtar, and soon came eggs and bunny rabbits. The Romans legalized Christianity, and the persecuted church, which was spreading the Gospel by being on the run, no longer needed to run and hide. They could now worship Christ and Caesar in a compromised manner dictated by Rome and its political authorities. The church backslid from there, the beginning of the Dark Ages, until roughly twelve centuries later and the Reformation, which came about with the invention of the printing press, thus enabling common men to read the Bible for themselves. In Revelation 2, Jesus warned the church that they had lost their "First Love" and needed to repent quickly by turning back to eat freely from the Tree of Life, Him. Regrettably, the church continued down the wrong path, and many books have been written throughout history about a number of moves of God, all of which began powerfully, yet ultimately morphed into lesser denominations (Some of these are now quite large numerically speaking.) or watered down humanistic versions of how they once started. I have heard the word "denomination" defined as a move of God that fizzled out. Still, I am so thankful that I met the Lord and became born again in one of these. The warning that Christ gave to the Ephesians was not heeded and, therefore today much of the church and its practices have become indifferent. At this juncture, I believe, we are exiting the Laodicean Church Age in Revelation 3, (referred to by Christ as the lukewarm church) and entering the Kingdom Age. (73)

When I first became born again, and read the Gospels and Acts with such a fresh passion, I often wondered why the Christian life which I now lived along with my friends did not mirror the mighty works of the saints in the book of Acts. God put an immense hunger in me to know Him and His word. This hunger not only inspired me to understand why I did or was asked to do anything in a so called church setting, but I also wanted understanding of everything spoken by those in authoritative leadership positions, yet I continued to wonder why the Bible seemed to read so differently than what transpired when we came together in our early meetings. In a sentence or two, I most firmly believe it is because the fire of the early Christians began to smolder in the fourth century. Christianity which once moved with the Holy Spirit, became watered down and increasingly more impacted by humanism. In Revelation 17 there is a woman with an inscription on her forehead that includes the words, "Mother of Harlots," who is seated on seven hills. (Rome does have seven hills.) In the Bible, Mother refers symbolically to the Church (think Jesus as the Bridegroom and we as His bride), so the mother of harlots is representative of the leader or origin of the false church. I once believed that the Mother is Catholicism and the harlots are her offspring or all the Protestant denominations that came mostly after the Reformation. I used to feel strongly about this until I was awakened (by an experience with Jesus) that all Christians are in this together and whether we are Catholic, Protestant, non-denominational, so called followers of Jesus, or whatever; we have all been influenced by the demonic, religious, pharisaical principalities that have come to steal our relationship with Christ, and replace it with some conformational Marxist institutional form of a religion or philosophy, not a Christ-centered way of abundant living, thinking, and being. We have taught our family that Christ did not come to bring Christianity, and that it is not a compliment to be referred to as exceptionally religious. The term Christian is used only twice in the Bible (74), and it was mostly a derogatory term non-Christians used to describe followers of The Way. (Jesus) Yet also understand that in James 1 the Bible references a true religion that is about helping the widows and orphans and keeping ourselves spotless before the Lord. Jesus taught late in His ministry that the greatest commandment is to love God with all of your heart, soul, and mind, and to love your neighbor as yourself (Matthew 22:36-40). For that reason, there has been a decade's long movement from "lukewarm" programmed assemblies, or forms of the true church, to divine, real, sincere families centered upon relationship with God and each other, founded upon sacrificial love to those whom God connects us relationally.

Importantly though, God has used these Catholic and Protestant institutions, and again, I met the Lord in one myself, and am forever thankful for my unquestionably needed path of spiritual upbringing. Father God knows what He is doing and can use anything or anybody to bring about His purposes. Upon reflection, for us, more so initially but also each time my family felt called to move, we felt that we had to overcome the fear of man (opposite of a Godly fear) that confronted us. The several church moves that we had were preceded by dreams and other revelation to do so, and each move brought us progressively to a new place to both get something the Lord knew that we desperately needed and also later to impart what we had to our new church families, so that we could all grow in Him. This growth should be about ever-increasing love, a becoming rather than doing, and as a result, although not a focus, an ever increasing influence as well, always moving forward with God, a transformation into his love, nature, and likeness (Gospel of the Kingdom). Unfortunately, we have learned that most Christians, upon the revelation of a higher way, stay right where they are, comfortably, rather than fight the resistance from peers and family. Especially in the city that I reside in now, a terrible competition exists among many of the pastors of the different assemblies here. I use the word "assembly" rather than "church," because the Bible teaches in Ephesians 4 that there is only one church. Still, we need the diversity that different local fellowships (or tribes / families) of believers bring as communities to create each church or city for our God. The biblical New Jerusalem is a picture of that city.

As I write this the world is experiencing an enormous threat from ISIS. I've learned and believe that the two biggest threats in our day to Christianity are radical Islam and Marxism. I have written above about the insidious demonic impact of Marxism to all Christians, by allowing us to believe that we get closer to God or obtain salvation through conforming and belonging to a like-minded group, or participating in ritualistic liturgical soundings, sacraments, and human engineered worship. The error here is most subtle, since community or family is so important to our fellowship. The focus has to be conforming to Him, not a group, movement, or denomination. If satan came to steal, kill, and destroy, it makes sense to me that any religion not about our one true God (Jesus) has to be an instrument of darkness, and satan will ultimately steal, kill, and destroy (John 10:10). Islam (or any other false religion) will therefore birth and breed radical Islam and other false forms of the one true Way, with the intent to destroy anything that does not join with it, through fear, hatred, and intimidation, and insidiously by any means possible.

It is partly because of these two major threats to Christianity and even our lives, that the church will mature to defeat their enemy. We will need great darkness in order to awaken to our own destiny, by overcoming this sin and culture of our day and whatever makes us fearful and threatens us. Through this maturation process I believe we will come to understand the importance of why God has His feasts in the Bible. I also believe that the celebration of the feasts of the Lord will be restored to the church with the harvest at the end of the age, when Jew and Gentile come together to form, according to Paul's writings, the one new man, in communion with Christ and each other (spiritual Israel, the New Jerusalem); picture the cross. (75) However, upon the permanent "return" of Christ on Earth, the feasts become unnecessary once we have all that matters, Christ our Bridegroom, Himself.

HOW THE BIBLE ONE DAY MADE PERFECT SENSE TO ME

It was with an understanding of the feasts of God and especially the three "mandatory" feasts that a light bulb turned on inside me, and all of a sudden the Bible made so much more sense. While before the Old Testament was more historical and seemingly for Israel and Jewish people, and the New Testament for Christians under the new covenant, now I could see Jesus throughout the whole Bible in this symbology, mystery, and hidden message about the history (think His story) of God's people. This revelation makes it abundantly clear for any inspired reader of the Bible of God's immeasurable love and multi-generational long-term plans for His people. The awakening to His love and life He had in store for me so helped to put my experiences in perspective, as well as a rudimentary grasp of His plans for me and His family in the days and years to come. This plan encompasses a "restoration of all things" lost (temporarily), yet also an ultimate sustainable move of God that goes far beyond anything the world has ever known. The foundation, I believe, is simply knowing God, Him and Emmanuel residing within hungry believers with whom He desires to partner.

Adam and Eve walked with God in the garden as son and daughter until their fall, yet when the veil of the temple was torn with the death of Jesus, our access to Papa was once again made available. Even still there are quite a few characters in the Old Testament that had the most intimate relationship with our God. A few examples are Enoch and Noah, both of whom the Bible declares as having "walked with God." In Numbers Chapter 12 Moses wrote about himself by quoting God, "as for my servant Moses I speak to him face to face...in the form of a Man." (Jesus) The Lord

Jesus told the Pharisees that Moses wrote about Him (John 5:46).

REVISITING EXODUS 12 AND LIKENING THIS PASSAGE TO MY LIFE

The Lord Jesus had a love for the Pharisees, Israel, and all of the world, so much so that He gave everything that He had, including every single day of His own life. His Father had foretold this life through His Son in Exodus 12. Recall that after Israel had moved to Goshen, rescued by Joseph in Egypt, great oppression came upon this people with a new leader who had fear of this great nation. Moses had been sent by God to free His people. Finally, after ten plagues, the last of which was prophetically darkness, Moses led Israel from Egypt, but not before God mandated a feast that was to be practiced forever. The Lord instructed Moses who instructed Israel, just before the great exodus from Egypt, to obtain a lamb without defect, inspect it for four days, and sacrifice it the night before their departure. There was to be one lamb per household. Once sacrificed, its blood was to be smeared on the sides and top of the door frames of each house. Each family then had to roast the lamb, including its entrails and head, and eat the entire lamb in haste, while fully dressed, ready to depart Egypt quickly. This feast was termed the Lord's Passover and was a day to "remember...a law for all time...a permanent law." (76) During the night a death angel visited every house in Egypt and if the doorposts were not painted the home experienced the loss of their firstborn child and the firstborn of any livestock. Pharoah, his officials, and the people woke up in the night to the sound of wailing and the realization that every Egyptian house experienced a death. He then sent for Moses and Aaron and commanded them to get out of Egypt, but before they left, they were given clothing, gold, and silver after asking the people of Egypt for these treasures. Foreigners living among the Israelites who had been circumcised were permitted to partake of the Passover and the exodus from Egypt.

The symbology here should be obvious to all Christians and peoples, and for this reason -- God had this scribed as part of His inspired Word. He also mandated the keeping of this feast for all Israel until Christ came. This symbology pointed to the day that Papa would send His Son to be the Passover Lamb, so that anyone who believed upon Him would have an everlasting and abundant life and be born into His family. For me, I have already written that my born-again experience began in my brokerage office with the realization that I had seen an answer to prayer for the first time in my life. I had made my exodus from spiritual Egypt, from the slavery, bondage, and oppression of spiritual darkness. I had become a new creation in Christ, made righteous and justified by my faith in Him. I was now ready to enter a land flowing with milk and honey. I now belonged to Papa and His family, and no longer was the property of Satan and Egypt. He placed a new nature in me, and a hunger for His Word, of which I could not get enough. Remember that the Israelites had to eat the entire lamb, in haste, fully clothed, while standing in their sandals. Likewise, when I became born again, Papa placed a hunger in me to eat and embrace ALL of His Word, and Him. Recollect that Jesus was called the Lamb of God and the Word of God which became flesh and dwelt among us (John Ch. 1). He told His followers that they were to eat His flesh and drink His blood, a remark that made most of them leave Him. The same is true today with most, especially those who embrace dispensationalism or secessionism, don't believe in miracles, or simply understand the Truth, but choose not to embrace It/Him. But this is foretold by Jewish historians as well, that only a remnant of Israel escaped the woes of Egypt. Yet even then God "so loved the world" that He provided a way out for foreigners who had been circumcised and partook of the Passover. In the book of John, Jesus said, "I am the door." It was symbolic of His blood that had to be painted on the sides and top of the door; this was a picture of Him, Jesus the Door, and His bloody cross. You and I must enter in through The Door; those in Exodus who did not, perished.

Also, of tremendous significance to me was that there was one animal chosen for each family for the first Passover. It could also have been a goat and not a sheep, symbolic of God's love for "all the world", both the sheep and the goats (see Matthew 25). Something Messianic Jews, I believe, understand far better than others, is that once a person becomes born again, it is for their entire household. This is evidenced, again, by instruction from God to have one lamb sacrificed for each household. We have testimony of this in Acts 10 with the entire family of Cornelius becoming born again, all at the same time. Also, very noteworthy is that for smaller families they could combine households if their family was too small to eat an entire lamb. This instruction foretold the salvation of God's family through partnership with one another. The Lord's army is clearly stronger in unity than divided; and His cross is a picture of the communion or common union of His body, first with Him, then Him found in all those around us.

Important also to revisit was the instruction from God to get the leaven out of every house and start another feast that coincided with Passover, called the Feast of Unleavened Bread. Additionally, Christ was raised on the Feast of First-Fruits which coincides with Unleavened Bread. This pointed to Christ as unleavened or without sin, the same way Papa sees us once we go through our exodus or Passover experience. Think about and picture this -- God sent His Son to Earth in a man suit, fully human, with no divine or special privileges...to show all humanity, by example, The Way to Life. (77) During His life, he became so unleavened by the daily trials, persecution, and sufferings, that by the time He died on the cross, it was God Himself dying for all whom He loved, even those who hated and killed Him. Since He is the Resurrection, and also the First-Fruit of many brethren, by His acts we can now enter into the resurrection or new way of abundant living as a new creation. Again, Passover was actually a feast comprised of three feasts of the Lord, and the first three of seven which Israel celebrated in perpetuity. When I reflect upon my own life I think of Passover, Unleavened Bread, and First-Fruits as pointing to, not just a coming out of Egypt or darkness, but a death, burial, and resurrection with Christ. Upon our death to our self (the old man), we are buried in baptism, and resurrected as a new creation. Upon Christ's death, the Bible reports that He went into Sheol, His burial gave all of the people who had gone before Him an opportunity to embrace Him, and a partnering for His resurrection three days later. (78) So, we die with Christ, are buried with Him in baptism, and are resurrected as a new creation into His family.

Prophetically, in Exodus, we see this death as a coming out of Egypt, followed by the Feast of Unleavened Bread, in order to get the leaven or the sin out; this was followed by a baptism in the Red Sea (the sea of Christ's blood at the cross), before Israel was resurrected to a new beginning in a land flowing with milk and honey. For me, the Lord instructed me to have a biblical baptism which I had in Venezuela. It was imperative to me to be baptized in the name of Jesus; He is the Name of the Father, Son, and Holy Spirit. A final revelation of the exodus as it relates to my experience, is to point out that Moses instructed everyone to inspect their lambs from the tenth day of the month until the fourteenth. These four days, I believe, were representative of 4000 years, from Adam to Christ; Papa trying to show us the Way for a restoration to the intimacy that was lost with the first Adam yet resurrected through the second Adam, Christ. Also noteworthy to me was that with every plague prior to the exodus, Moses requested permission for a three-day excursion into the wilderness to have a feast to his God. I believe that the three days has twofold significance: one, the three days prior to Christ's resurrection; and the third day which began 2000 years (the third day is the third 1000 year period) after Christ, a millennium that we enter into after our wilderness experience.

SIGNIFICANCE TO CHRISTIAN BELIEVERS

About a year ago I was at work and walked downstairs to get some coffee when I heard the Lord speak to me and say that the feasts of God foretold the death, burial, and resurrection of the Lamb of God, beginning in Exodus 12 -- so that Father God's chosen people (Israel) could be saved. Then with Christ He made the chosen status available to any son or daughter on Earth, any descendent of Abraham, so that all of the families on Earth, all descendants (spiritual Israel) of Abraham could be blessed by knowing God.

What is so amazing about God's timeless inspired written word, the Bible, is how every book is a treasure that points to Messiah, Jesus. God told Abraham in Genesis 12 that all of the families of the Earth would be blessed through him. Abraham was not Jewish; he fathered Ishmael (Islam), and Isaac, from whom both Muslims and Jews, and ultimately Gentiles could know God by believing in His Son.

I recently shared this with a Christian friend who found difficulty understanding that Christians are really spiritual Jews. He confessed to an understanding that the Old Testament was mostly written for followers of Judaism and the New Testament for Christians. But again, every book of the Bible was divinely written by God's Holy Spirit, through inspired writers, to point all of mankind to Jesus so that through faith every walking, breathing human could have what Adam had in the Garden of Eden. An understanding of the feasts supernaturally shows any sincere reader, regardless of race, nationality, sex, etc., that Jesus came to set us all free from bondage and any problems, to instead live a phenomenally abundant life centered upon intimately knowing Him so that we could love all those around us.

Jesus came to show us the relationship that we are meant to have with Papa which is so beautifully illustrated by the mandatory feasts of the Lord found in the Old Testament: The Feast of Unleavened Bread, The Feast of Weeks or Pentecost, and The Feast of Tabernacles/ Ingathering or Booths. It took me a long time as a new believer to understand the importance of the Old Testament, so much so that I didn't think that I needed to read it. While the four Gospels provide a foundation for the believer, I have discovered over and over that the Old Testament foretells and points to the Lord Jesus in many places. There are quite a few people in the Old Testament that knew the Lord Jesus. For some readers, this may seem hard to believe so please bear with me.

CONTINUING TO PARALLEL MY EXPERIENCE WITH ISRAEL AND THE EARLY CHURCH

So reflecting back upon my born again experience, my exodus from Egypt, my beginning as a new creation in Christ, an awakening from the spiritual coma that I had been in, recall that having felt the call of God on my life, I immediately began the facilitation of the 112 group, our Bible study. While this study lasted five years, sixteen months into it my second encounter (The Encounter) with the Lord occurred. I had been diligently seeking Him mostly through His Word for more than a year, in hindsight without the fullness of the power of His Holy Spirit. It was on that morning, standing in the stairwell with Mike, when the Holy Spirit came upon us in love and power. That afternoon we prayed for the man in the coma. This was my Pentecost.

PENTECOST IN THE
OLD TESTAMENT

Most biblical scholars associate the first Pentecost
with the giving of the law to Israel in Exodus 19.
Moses went up to God after He had called him
from the mountain and the Lord recalled to Moses
how "I bore you on eagles' wings," what He did to
the Egyptians and that He was bringing Israel to
Himself. (v.4) In verse six He said that they would
be to Him a kingdom of priests and a holy nation.
He had Moses sanctify Israel in order to prepare
them for the Lord to speak on the third day. On the
morning of the third day there were thunderings
and lightnings coming from a thick cloud on the
mountain. Mount Sinai was completely in smoke,
because the Lord descended upon it in fire. The
whole mountain quaked greatly, and the people of
Israel were terrified of God's awesome power.
Moses was on top of the mountain speaking to
God when He instructed him to warn the people
not to break through to gaze at Him, so that they
would not perish. He then told him to ensure that

the priests consecrate themselves. Moses replied that the people could not come up, so the Lord said, "Away," and told Moses to get down and then bring Aaron, his brother, back up with him. After he descended the mountain the Lord used him to give Israel the Ten Commandments.

I believe that God had intended this Pentecost to be the birth of His "kingdom of priests," but Israel was not ready for this intimacy with God, so he gave them the law. This was meant to be the birth of the church of God, but ultimately every Jew that had gone through the Exodus, with the exception of Joshua and Caleb, died in the wilderness over the next 40 years. While sad, everything that God does is redemptive, and He had Israel celebrate Pentecost, also termed the Feast of Weeks, for the next 1500 years before the real birth of the church in Acts 2. (See also Revelation 12, "Now a great sign appeared in heaven: a woman clothed with the sun (Son)...She bore a male child...") In Leviticus 23:16 God made mandatory the practice of celebrating Pentecost "the morrow after the 7th Sabbath" after the Feast of First Fruits," (exactly 50 days after Passover) which every able-bodied Jewish male had to attend in Jerusalem.

ACTS 2

1500 years later Jesus told his disciples and a remnant of His followers to tarry in Jerusalem until they be endued with power from on high. He told them that they would be baptized with the Holy Spirit "not many days from now," and that they would receive power when the Holy Spirit "has come upon you."   These sayings had been previously foretold by John the Baptist who said, "I indeed baptize you with water, but One mightier than I is coming, whose sandal strap I am not worthy to loose. He will baptize you with the Holy Spirit and fire." So, when the day of Pentecost had fully come the 120 in the upper room were filled with the Holy Spirit and began to speak in tongues, which were understood by "every nation under heaven." Peter then referenced Joel 2 regarding an outpouring of God's Holy Spirit, followed by his first sermon, a powerful revealing of Christ, in which 3000 men, not counting women and children, were born again.

On this day a mighty redemptive restoration of what had happened in Exodus 19 had begun. This was the birthing of God's "kingdom of priests," a family of God, that could now know Him intimately with the power of His Holy Spirit that now resided within all who believed. This was the baptism of the Holy Spirit, a baptism by Christ, which was accompanied with great boldness and resurrection power, a witness of all that Christ had accomplished on Earth, especially His resurrection. The message that Peter gave was not from the same Peter who had denied Christ three times. This Peter, the apostle to the Jewish church, now had Jesus FULLY residing within him.

This baptism of love and power, foretold in Joel 2 and Exodus 19, jump started and began God's family / church "on Earth as it is in heaven," in Acts 2, and a little more than 2000 years ago. It was the power of God's indwelling Holy Spirit that came upon Mike and me while we stood at that stairwell before we prayed for helpless David who was in the coma. That was the first day of my encounter that I am writing about here, which began a 40-day period that I will never forget, though at the time, I had no idea what had happened to either of us; we did not understand that there even was a pentecostal baptism from Jesus. (79) But the Lord's timing was perfect because we were able to enter that hospital room with a boldness that neither of us had before, and the resurrection power of Christ residing within us, for a mission that had to be accomplished that afternoon.

I had been justified by my belief in God sixteen months prior, but my awakening and ability to communicate with my Maker had gone up about tenfold from where I had been. I can only recall a few times prior to this baptism of hearing God's voice. But now with this empowerment I had it within me to receive my daily bread, "to eat His flesh and drink His blood," devour the Word, both written and spoken, and potentially know what it was that I was to do each day, if I were to seek Him out to understand His bread for me, each morning when I awakened. The evidence of this baptism was an increase in boldness, power, His love, and spectacular unstoppable joy, my strength. A deeper understanding and realization of Him residing within me greatly upgraded my faith and desire to please my Maker, my First Love, above all others. It was with this empowerment that I could now have a greater relationship with God, even a most meaningful friendship, so that I could begin a brand new, refreshing existence with Him and everybody else. At the time I did not have any perspective like now that we would soon be entering our wilderness experience with Him, a time to hear His voice so that I could become mature and sanctified, unleavened and more like His Son, God on Earth in a man suit, and grow in our relationship each day, by seeking Him, and even face to face interactions with Jesus. Consider this awesome promise from Christ, "...And he who loves Me will be loved by My Father, and I will love him and manifest (show and reveal) Myself to him." (80) Paul wrote many Scriptures about "the return of the Lord." These inspired writings were not about the end of the Age, but about Christ revealing Himself to the hungry ones then and now!

THE WILDERNESS

Having come through Pentecost we now have it in us to seek Him early and often in order to receive our daily bread, or what it is that He would have us to do. Upon entering our wilderness experience though, we enter into a number of long, difficult trials, the duration of which cause us to suffer much longer than we could have initially imagined. The Lord becomes sneaky and, at times, difficult to hear, especially amongst the multitude of other misleading thoughts and voices. (Reference Job's friends who were completely missing God about his trial in the Book of Job.) He feels distant but He is always there with us and His peace that passes all human understanding and reason. In other words, our situation is troublesome and does not feel quite right. At times it feels like we are barely moving forward with no guidance or direction, blind. Herein is why we sheep must truly know the voice our great Shepherd so clearly.

Consider the blind man from Bethesda in Mark 8. His friends brought him to Jesus to be touched or healed, their way. But the Lord took him instead, most uncharacteristically, out of town, out of his comfort zone, void of his friends and all familiarity. He then spit on His eyes and asked how he could see. Imagine hearing from Papa that you are to spit on someone to heal them. Jesus was "flying blind," totally submitted to the will of His Father. When the man responded that things were fuzzy Jesus laid His hands on him and told Him to look up. Once the man looked towards the heavens he could see clearly....but, he had to get way out of his comfort zone in order to be victorious in this heretofore lifelong struggle. He had to "fly blind" in order to see clearly.

In studying the Bible and church history, I believe that there were few believers who successfully navigated this wilderness walk and entered into His rest, the Promised Land. Since Jesus is the Promise, if we can enter into Him, we can enter into these promises, our inheritance that awaits us from Papa. There is a prophetic picture in the Old Testament of Israel attempting to enter into this rest, a land flowing with milk and honey, The Promised Land which they never obtained (with the exception of Enoch). Instead, they wandered helplessly around their wilderness until Christ came. An exception to this is the Joshua generation which did cross the Jordan and enter into His promises. However, their newfound liberties were short-lived and Israel's dominion and walk with God fizzled back to their old ways. With

Christ Israel became "spiritual Israel" and there were some in the first century church who became "perfected" in the Lord, fully mature sons and daughters of their living God. (81) However, soon afterwards the church once again fell away, entered into the dark ages, and church history indicates that, with few exceptions, even the pentecostal, baptisms of power ceased until the church began to reawaken in the nineteenth century.

I mention this because once we become born again and filled with His spirit, we enter into our wilderness, our valley, just like Christ did (immediately following His baptism by John and before the start of His ministry), and stay there until we enter into maturity. Every believer must go through this experience so that we may become less, a death to ourselves and our will, and more like Him. In Exodus 23:28, the Lord is quoted by Moses talking about Him, sending hornets before the Israelites to drive out their enemies. He said in verses 29 and 30, "I will not drive them out from before you in one year, lest the land become desolate and the beasts of the field become too numerous for you. Little by little I will drive them out from before you, until you have increased, and you inherit the land." Our wilderness experience requires patience as the Lord deals with us little by little, giving us no more than we can handle, so that our hearts die to our flesh and we become readied for our inheritance which is the Promised Land depicted by the final "mandatory" feast, Tabernacles. Our greatest opportunity is in this wilderness, valley, or trial, where every temptation is an opportunity to hear God. For me, He is also waking me up to fear only Him and no man or anything else. Again, for centuries believers have remained, just like Israel, in the wilderness, trying (not hard enough), yet also not fully committed to know God and enter into what Enoch and some, like the apostles in the Gospels did and became, in the first century.

Ironically, Israel's wilderness walk took forty years. What makes this unusual is that their journey was only 250 miles, a distance that could be easily walked in a dozen days or less. Our time spent in this experience is determined by how long it takes us to die, or get rid of all of our baggage, the negative fruit found in Galatians; whether we make it in one day or moment, or never do. We can be greatly encouraged by the life of Mary Magdalene, having been possessed by seven demons, she had one encounter with Christ, yet followed Him all the way to the cross. Only John of the Twelve did not scatter with the others.

For me, it has now been seventeen years since my pentecostal experience, the beginning of my encounter, all of which I can describe as wandering around in life and wishing that I could get back to that place I experienced seventeen years ago, and stay there, or better yet, continue to move forward, with Him. However, recall that it took the disciples more than three and a half years personally with Jesus before they entered into the Promise of fully "knowing" God and His ways. Only in the last year have I come to understand so much more about this walk in my wilderness. A revelation that recently struck me was that through both the extreme ups and downs in our walk with God, He has always been there, with and for us. Just like the sparrow, the raven, or the flower, He provides all that we need. At times, for me, thinking economically or provisionally, and with other difficult types of trials, it seems that there is no way out. I mean that. However, in my life, He has always come through. Only recently have I come to count on and understand that He is, and has always been my Provision, my Promise...just like when Israel crossed the Red Sea, they were given quail and manna for 40 years. We really lack nothing in the wilderness because God is with us; we just don't always recognize that He is so faithful to provide for us. He even fights our battles for us. There is an exceptionally small remnant that will follow the narrow Path and make it into the

Promised Land; they will know their Father so well, that they will be able to make their own provision, without even thinking about their needs. When Joshua and Caleb and the ten spies entered into the Promised Land in Numbers 13 they found grapes, pomegranates, and figs in abundance. The grapes were so large that they could only put one cluster on a pole which was carried by Joshua and Caleb. It is this land flowing with milk and honey, across the Jordan River, which the Lord permitted me to taste for forty days during my encounter with Him.

Romans 14:17 reads…"for the kingdom of God is not eating and drinking, but righteousness, and peace and joy in the Holy Spirit." Jesus told us in the Sermon on the Mount (Matthew 6:33), to "seek first the kingdom of God and His righteousness, and all these things shall be added to you." If we capitalize Righteousness, we are seeking Jesus, with all of our might, and we enter into Him, the Promise, or Promised Land, the milk and honey, all of these wonderful things which "shall be added to [us]." I was able to taste, drink, even devour, this milk and honey during my encounter, which brought more peace, and especially joy, than I have ever experienced. Nothing in life compares to this joy, these feelings, this resonating Love from within, that smothered me and made me feel like something precious encapsulated within a cocoon...this Love that has never left me, and caused "rivers of living water to flow out of my heart." While Righteousness and Peace come with Passover and Pentecost, Joy and every promise imaginable comes forth with the next feast, as we cross the Jordan River, and this spectacular, unimaginable Joy awakens and resides within our hearts. This is foretold biblically with the feast of Tabernacles, of which I had entered into, tasted and saw for myself, this goodness of God, His uninhibited love for me for 40 days.

TABERNACLES

Before starting with Tabernacles, a quick summary follows. Jesus was our Passover Lamb whom we embraced with our born again awakening once the Father had drawn us to Him; Jesus then baptizes the obedient and hungry ones with His Holy Spirit, love and power at Pentecost; and the awakening of our Spirit residing within us progresses through this process of simply knowing Him and Him through others whom we relationally connect during this sanctification process or death to self while walking under Papa's provision during our wilderness and valley experiences. In Tabernacles we enter all of the promises of the Father, and it is no longer we who live, but rather fully "Christ in us, the hope of glory." Jesus came to show us the Way, a narrow path to His Father whereby we become one with Him. Our model is the straight line that Jesus followed as the First-Fruits of many brethren, yet a remnant that like Jesus, walks so closely with God that we only do the will of our Father on planet Earth. While "wide is the path to destruction", this very slim path ultimately leads us to a place where Jesus within us becomes more, and through many persecutions and never ending trials, with His help we reach oneness, a state described by Paul in Galatians 2; "I am crucified with Christ, nevertheless I live, yet not I, and the life which I now live, I live by the faith of the Son of God, who loved me and gave Himself for me." Passover, Pentecost ...Tabernacles, where we have been transfigured into His likeness, becoming one with the Father.

At approximately 520 B.C., the prophet Zechariah wrote, "And it shall come to pass that everyone who is left of all the nations which came against Jerusalem shall go up from year to year to worship the King, the Lord of hosts, and to keep the Feast of Tabernacles. And it shall be that whichever of the families of the earth do not come up to Jerusalem to worship the King, the LORD of hosts, on them there will be no rain. If the family of Egypt will not come up and enter in, they shall have no rain; they shall receive the plague with which the LORD strikes the nations who do not come up to keep the Feast of Tabernacles. This shall be the punishment of Egypt and the punishment of all the nations that do not come up to keep the Feast of Tabernacles. In that day "HOLINESS TO THE LORD" shall be engraved on the bells of the horses. The pots in the LORD's house shall be like the bowls before the altar. Yes, every pot in Jerusalem and Judah shall be holiness to the LORD of hosts. Everyone who sacrifices shall come and take them and cook in them. In that day there shall no longer be a Canaanite in the house of the LORD of hosts." (82)

This spectacular Scripture gives us a picture of this Feast of Tabernacles, a passage that foretells a glimpse of what it will be like to walk in Oneness with the Lord Jesus as we walk with and follow Him, in harmony with all believers. In Matthew 25 we see all the nations gathered before Him and separated into sheep on His right and goats on His left. This separation is paralleled in Zechariah where all the people, cities, and nations that had come out of Egypt are now so joyously following King Jesus to Jerusalem for this great festival. The pots in the Lord's house, us, are earthen vessels that have sacrificed and yielded to the will of our Lord until we have reached this never before witnessed level of unity and maturity, the Lord's family. The Canaanites, little gods or idols within our hearts and thinking until now had never been completely rooted out, yet now is left a company of overcoming peoples who are no longer double minded followers of self, but completely in tune to the Spirit and the will of Father, to whom Jesus came to Earth to lead us.

This passage is both spiritual and occurs in the natural. While the law required Israel to keep this once mandatory feast, in this passage we see Jesus's sold out followers walking to Jerusalem, the geographical center and city of our God and His people, both in the Spirit daily and in joy and celebratory fashion once a year, riding on horseback alongside our Lord and King, a company of believers so close, willing to die for Jesus, and one another, in communion, a common union of having partnered with Him and each other in our daily lives.

Again, the endpoint to this walk or lifelong journey is Christ in us, the hope of glory, and being crucified and becoming one with Him (Galatians 2:20). All that we have to do is know His will and be radically obedient. These feasts explain and illustrate a wonderful path to the Father for every believer and serve to show the natural branch (Israel) their Bridegroom and Messiah. Jesus came to show spiritual Israel, Jew and Gentile as one, this way to Himself and the Father. With understanding of what the feasts represent we can be more postured in celebration, praise, and thanksgiving, for all that He has done for us. The final feast, Tabernacles, also referred to as Ingathering or Booths, broadly covers the Feast of

Trumpets, the Day of Atonement, and The Feast of Tabernacles.

TRUMPETS

Joshua and Israel had just celebrated Passover as they overlooked Jericho, an arid land and heavily fortified city. The children of Israel were no longer fed manna from heaven but made and found their own provision here in the Promised Land. The Lord instructed Israel's army and priests to march around the city seven days in a row. The first six, the priests blew trumpets, ram's horns or shofars, as they circled the city one time, the Ark of the Lord carried behind the priests. On the seventh day, they encircled the city seven times while, again, seven priests blew trumpets. On the seventh lap, when the horns sounded, Joshua instructed Israel to shout, "For the Lord has given you the city." They then shouted with a great shout; the walls fell down flat; they ran into the city, destroyed everything and everybody, and kept all of the silver and gold. (See Joshua 7.)

It is amazing to me how most Christian families teach this story to their children at such a young age, but most probably never see all of the symbology here, myself included. In the Old Testament Israel, trumpets were blown when it was time to come in from the field of work to go to the tabernacle. They were sounded when Israel needed to move or go to battle. In Jericho the rams' horns were blown, symbolically, to awaken the church, God's most intimate family, for what was about to take place. His people were entering into a land given to them, inherited from Papa, a place flowing with milk and honey, produce, and great spoils for the taking. After centuries in captivity, toiling in Egypt and the wilderness, Israel could now be deliriously happy with eternal joy.

Symbolically, this land is a place of rest that we enter into in our hearts and is about to take place, evidenced by the Feast of Tabernacles which is upon the church, after Trumpets. Note that all Israel, in communion with one another and obedient to God's instruction, shouted in unison at Jericho, with all their might, as seven trumpets sounded, and the Ark followed the priests. The trumpets had awakened the church for what was before them. This is a sound or a Voice that we must hear to enter our Rest. The seven laps on the seventh day with seven priests foretells the church entering into a time of perfection (seven), the Lord's Rest, and also the seventh day or millennium, the beginning of a one-thousand-year period since Adam. When we are postured to hear His voice and do, our faith and hope increase, and the walls come down so we can be intimate and vulnerable with each other, divine connections desperately needed. So, Trumpets is a time of increased hearing, and thus understanding, a preparation for God's best, as we prepare to enter into Tabernacles and heaven on Earth. Where in Isaiah 55, He tells us that His ways and thoughts are higher than ours, we now have an invitation to know His ways because we know Him. It is as if Papa is saying and sounding to all on our planet and in the heavenlies, "Here comes My glorious church, My bride, My beloved sons and daughters in whom I am well pleased. Get ready, they are coming. Wake up!" Before we enter in, however, we have one most serious day of preparation called Atonement.

THE DAY OF ATONEMENT

The Day of Atonement which follows, is a heightened revelatory period for those who seek Him, a day of reflection, celebration, repentance, and an acknowledgement of Jesus' atoning sacrificial act. Before Christ, or before the Lamb was slain, on this day, the high priest of Israel entered the fearsome Holy of Holies, where God Himself dwelt. One time each year, the priest made the atoning sacrifice for all Israel. Both then and now (for those who are called and understand) this day is considered the highest of the holy days. Today, the Lord's prophets and true shepherds wait on Him during these 24 hours in order to get their part in discerning what God is doing with His church in the coming year. But 3500 years ago, God's people were under His law. In Exodus 20 where Moses was given the 10 Commandments, those who worshiped other gods were subject to a seemingly horrific curse, that our "jealous God would visit the iniquity of the fathers upon the children to the third and fourth generations of those who hated Him." However, our most merciful Father soon gave Israel a way out for their sins, a wiping the slate clean, annually, through sacrifice and repentance during the Day of Atonement. Because of The Atonement, Christ, we have been washed and cleansed by His blood, and with each year and celebration of this feast, we move closer to perfection and becoming one with the Lord, which points to Tabernacles. Jesus' fulfillment of Tabernacles was His becoming one with His Father, and remember that He came to Earth as a man with no special or divine privileges. The fulfillment for the believer is His coming through us, our death to self and our will, transfiguring into His likeness, and becoming one with Our Father and His will, where He tabernacles in us. Also called Booths, imagine the most closely-knit family of God tabernacling with one another, an ingathering in small, most intimate booths or shelters, in order to do the will of Papa. Jesus has shown us the way; He is that Way, the Lord of the Sabbath, the seventh day of Rest, into whom we must enter.

TABERNACLES, BOOTHS, OR INGATHERING

Lastly, we read about the final of the three mandatory feasts in Leviticus 23:39-43, "Also on the fifteenth day of the seventh month, when you have gathered in the fruit of the land, you shall keep the feast of the Lord for seven days; on the first day there shall be a Sabbath-rest, and on the eighth day a Sabbath-rest. And you shall take for yourselves on the first day the fruit of beautiful trees, branches of palm trees, the boughs of leafy trees, and willows of the brook, and you shall rejoice before the Lord your God for seven days.

You shall keep it as a feast to the Lord for seven days in the year. It shall be a statute forever in your generations. You shall celebrate it in the seventh month. You shall dwell in booths for seven days. All who are native Israelites shall dwell in booths, that your generations may know that I made the children of Israel dwell in booths when I brought them out of the land of Egypt: I am the Lord your God."

Again, in Deuteronomy we read, "You shall observe the Feast of Tabernacles seven days, when you have gathered from your threshing floor and from your winepress. And you shall rejoice in your feast, you and your son and your daughter, your male servant and your female servant and the Levite, the stranger and the fatherless and the widow, who are within your gates. Seven days you shall keep a sacred feast to the Lord your God in the place which the Lord chooses, because the Lord your God will bless you in all your produce and in all the work of your hands, so that you surely rejoice."

The Feast of Tabernacles, also called Ingathering, or Booths was a time of celebration for entire Jewish families after the harvest. They were instructed to gather together in booths while they partook of the feast for seven days. On the first day of Tabernacles we had a Sabbath day of rest followed by seven days of the feast and finally another day of rest. In Hebrews 4:11 we have a command to diligently seek to enter the Lord's rest; He is that Rest. What Tabernacles represents in the Bible is a time where we have gotten so close to Father God that He tabernacles within us. He does not reside in buildings made with hands, but inside of us. This feast represents the high call of the Lord and the fullness of what it means to be a son or daughter of God. The manifestation of Booths in our lives is the fulfillment of the prayer of Jesus to Father God in the garden of Gethsemane, that we together, would be one with the Father.

Deuteronomy 32:30 states that one can put a thousand to flight but two, ten thousand. Herein lies His kingdom's powerful mathematics of family and relationships.

Jesus came to show us the way to the Father. The Father is representative of Tabernacles. While I have had a partial revelation of Tabernacles, this is something that really has not ever happened in America, and you must go back to the first century church to see this in the Bible, in the book of Acts. Those who partake of Tabernacles are the overcomers of God who are mentioned with each of the seven churches in Revelation, chapters two and three. The Lord Jesus was speaking to the false church and also to the overcoming church who are a remnant sold out to the high calling of God that Paul wrote about, the Bride of Christ. The last day's church eats freely from the Tree of Life and ultimately comes to truly know Papa. Malachi saw the hearts of the sons turning to the Father. The Feast of Booths is about a family of God that is in community with one another and has been transfigured into His likeness. We see this in the Scriptures with three of the twelve disciples who went farther with the Lord than the others. Peter, James, and John witnessed the transfiguration which was representative of the manifestation of the sons of God on the earth once Jesus ascended. Jesus walked in Tabernacles after the dove descended upon Him when John baptized Him. The disciples became mature sons of the Father, tabernacling with Him after Pentecost. Jesus will fulfill this feast once again with His return to the earth to rule and reign with His sons and daughters. We will fulfill this feast with the fullness of Christ manifesting in and through us. Galatians 2:20 is a picture of the sold-out believer who has been baptized by fire which has burned up all of that within us that is not Him. "I have been crucified with Christ; it is no longer I who live, but Christ lives in me; and the life which I now live in the flesh I live by faith in the son of God, who loved me and gave Himself for me."

SONSHIP

Romans 8:18,19 reads, "For I consider that the sufferings of this present time are not worthy to be compared with the glory which shall be revealed in us, for the earnest expectation of the creation eagerly waits for the revealing of the sons of God." In verse 14 Paul writes that as many as are led by the Spirit of God, these are sons of God. C.S. Lewis, man of God and author, said that the Son of God became a man to enable men to become sons of God. Sonship is about knowing who your Father is. We have been adopted into the family of our Father God through His Son Jesus, just like the prodigal son who threw away all that he had, only to be so graciously received back into his father's arms. This walk is not about what we do but who we become and who we know. We are Father God's adopted kids, first little children, then young men, and finally mature fathers as well. All that is required is that we believe or trust and obey with all of our hearts. We have been created in the image and likeness of God. As we grow in spirit

226

with our co-heir, our partner and comforter, the Holy Spirit, we grow in our relationship with Papa and the family and community of God. We grow into mature sons and daughters as we overcome the trials that await us. In Revelation 21:7 we read, "He who overcomes shall inherit all things, and I will be his God and he shall be My son." This is that day that Papa says to all, "This is my beloved son in whom I am well pleased."

While every believer is a son or a daughter of Father God, the sons that we read about in Romans 8 are those who have gone onto maturity. These are the overcomers who have overcome the culture, darkness, and indifference of our day (See also Revelation 2 and 3.). Mature sons have been fully transfigured into Papa's image and likeness and carry the glory of God while walking the earth, Paul's "better resurrection." We get a picture of what the bride of Christ will look like on the earth in Matthew 17 when Jesus became transfigured. The last days Bride of Christ, the sons and daughters of God will be a remnant as evidenced by only three of the twelve: Peter, James, and John, walking out the most intimate relationship with the Lord. The only ones present at the transfiguration, with their Lord, they fully manifested faith, hope, and love.

After selfishness and self-centeredness the last obstacle for Christ's bride, his mature sons and daughters, to overcome is death itself, just like Paul stated that he did not care whether he lived or died. All of the twelve early apostles were martyred, I believe, with the exception of John. Peter did not feel worthy to be crucified upright, so he died this slow death upside down. At the end of John's epistle Christ foretells Peter's end in this realm, but hints that John may remain until His return, or never die. I've read reports that John was boiled in a large cauldron of oil and water, only to later walk away. He was exiled to the Island of Patmos where he wrote Revelation as an old man. Christ said in John 10, "I lay down My life for the sheep," and later, "Therefore My Father loves Me, because I lay down My life that I may take it again. No one takes it from Me, but I lay it down of Myself. I have power to lay it down, and I have power to take it again. This command I have received from My Father." (John 10:15-18) Once we fully enter in or become one with the Lord, no one can take our life from us unless Papa permits it. Do we love Jesus enough to willingly lay down our lives for our brothers and sisters, even if they don't like us?

Again, in Romans 8:14, Paul writes that ..."as many as are led by the Spirit of God, these are sons of God." "Sons" here in the Greek is translated from *"huios,"* which means fully mature, perfected men and women of God. Verse 15, "For you did not receive the spirit of bondage again to fear, but you received the Spirit of adoption by whom we cry out, Abba, Father." Verse 17 ..."and if children then heirs—heirs of God and joint heirs with Christ, if indeed we suffer with Him, that we may also be glorified together." Once we have been through Pentecost, or baptized by Jesus with His Holy Spirit, we have the Spirit of adoption residing deep within us, groaning and crying out for more, so much more, the full redemption of our body. (See verse 23.) All of creation is eagerly waiting for this coming day when a company of believers get so close to Papa and one-another that we see this feast of Booths / Ingathering / Tabernacles manifest on Earth, whereby the Spirit of adoption placed into us by Jesus becomes completely awakened to our true reality or identity. It is no longer us walking planet Earth, but fully Christ within us, and the faith OF our Daddy, Father God.

A PICTURE OF THE THREE FEASTS TOGETHER

Jesus is the Passover Lamb; The Holy Spirit is representative of Pentecost; And Tabernacles represents Father God, to whom Christ came to lead us.

At Passover we have come out of Egypt; during Pentecost we have a wilderness experience; and Tabernacles is about entering the Promised Land.

Christ came to show us The Way as a new creature in Christ; with the Holy Spirit at Pentecost we come to know the Truth; and through our wilderness and many trials we enter into the abundant Life at Tabernacles...The Way, The Truth, and The Life.

We are justified by Faith at Passover, obtain a greater Hope during Pentecost, and become Love in Booths.

At Passover we enter the peace of God; At Pentecost we receive power from on High; and at Booths we enter His Rest. Passover is representative of Peace from God; Pentecost, Peace with God; and Tabernacles, Peace of God. We are made righteous by the blood of the Lamb at Passover, obtain a greater peace at Pentecost; and become overflowing with joy at Tabernacles....For the kingdom of God is not about food or drink, but righteousness, peace, and joy in the Holy Spirit. The cross made us righteous; we are sanctified by the Holy Spirit and find a lasting peace; and real joy comes, in spite of any terrible life circumstances, when we fully know Papa. In the Old Testament we see Enoch who was a fully manifested son of God. He had overcome all things including himself, death itself, become one with the Father, and was ultimately raptured to another realm. With the last day's church, we shall again see the return of the Spirit of Elijah on the remnant, a company of people totally sold out to Christ.

BACK TO MY LIFE AND THE ENCOUNTER

While it took me years and lots of instruction to get this revelation, I was given the opportunity to experience this myself with the forty-day encounter that I had where again, I needed little or no sleep or food, and was cocooned, totally consumed in an atmosphere of love and life. Where the twelve disciples of the Lord continued to grow in Him throughout the rest of their lives on Earth, for me, over about the next hundred days the depth of the Holy Spirit that had come upon me began to very gradually leak out, until I became a more normal human being. Now, it is easy for me to see that the Lord meant for me to have a taste of this perfected "being" so that I could climb the mountain again during my life, and through the most difficult trials still have an incredible remembrance of where I am purposed to go, in Christ. He gave me a taste of the "end from the beginning." The reason why the eleven remaining apostles continued as fully manifested beloved sons of the Father was because they had been with Jesus for 42 months. While likely remote, I believe that it would have been possible for me to have stayed in this atmosphere myself forever;

however, I did not have a father, or likeminded friends in the Lord to guide me at that time like the disciples had, and my soul and mind were unsanctified. Without a father like Jesus it was so difficult to even do my job because all I cared about was spending time with the Lord and talking about Him to everyone during the day. This experience, again, totally consumed me. I believe that God's timing was perfect in this regard, and, of course, always is.

The other main issue to address is that once we go from Passover to Pentecost we have the Holy Spirit to guide and direct us, but most importantly to correct us when we sin and to help us clean up our soul so that we bear the fruit of the Spirit that Paul wrote about in Galatians 5. Because we haven't been discipled by the Lord like the disciples, we need the Lord's chosen earthly shepherd to point us to Christ and His ways. Also, we need a wilderness experience so that we learn obedience by the things that we suffer, and the mistakes that we make. We grow the most in this valley. Paul wrote that there were many teachers but not many fathers in the Lord. Malachi wrote about a day in his 4th chapter where the spirit of Elijah would return, and the hearts of the fathers would be turned to the children and the hearts of the children to the fathers. I believe that this season is upon us. In John's writing of 1st John he wrote of a progression in the life of the believer from little children to young men to fathers. Fathers were described as having known our true Father. The Christian life or walk is that simple, boiling down to just knowing God. In the quest to become a father, John further describes the Lord as Love, Light, and Life. As we grow in the Lord, we must become these three things.

This brings up another important point; that salvation, for many is the endpoint to the life of a believer. We have been taught that the Gospel is the good news about God's saving grace, so that we can go to heaven and become deliriously happy along with everyone else that has preceded us. But the Bible really teaches that this is only the beginning--for those who want all of God. How many times have we recited the Lord's Prayer on Sunday without really thinking about what we are saying, "Thy kingdom come, thy will be done, on earth as it is in heaven. Give us this day our daily bread..." My point is that we are called to get our bread every morning from heaven, know what we are supposed to do that day and walk it out with radical obedience, and in so doing bring heaven to Earth. The Bible states that the Lord is returning for a bride that is without spot or wrinkle. What if the second coming of Christ is about Him being fully manifested in us, the hope of glory, and heaven manifests wherever we go. When Peter walked the Earth, people were healed by his shadow. This was not his shadow, but the strongest anointing of God that rested upon Him and whacked anyone that got near him. Demons had to flee; sickness had to leave the atmosphere that he cultivated around himself, and people were changed by his presence, precisely like he had been taught by his mentor, the Lord Jesus.

THE KINGDOM AGE

What is so important to understand is all of the forces of God that are converging at this time on the Earth, all at the same time. We have the spirit of Elijah returning to bring about God's community and family through fathering; God's government that is written about in Ephesians 4 for the teaching, fathering, and maturation of the body of Christ that is coming back as well. This means that the apostolic governance which the church has not seen since the first century has to return before we can get back to the glorious church that we read about during the first century in the book of Acts. We are exiting the Church Age written about in Revelations 2 and 3, and entering the Kingdom Age, so that His Kingdom is prepared for the return of King Jesus on the earth for His Millennial reign.

While we have seen a few token believers experience Tabernacles / Booths, like Enoch and Elijah, we will see many that manifest as sons of the Father to usher in the great harvest at the end of the age, also referred to as the Feast of Ingathering in Exodus 23:16 where, "you have gathered in the fruit of your labors from the field." This speaks of the great harvest at the end of the age. We will see denominational walls come down and the church return to real community. The remnant that experiences the fullness of God also represents a true crossing of the Jordan River and entering into the Promised Land until Christ's return. God's government will be utilized in its fullness with the apostles and prophets working as the joint supplied with Christ as the Head.

Unless we return to our First Love (see Rev. 2), we will not see the subtle manner in which satan has made inroads and tricked the Church. Once in deep, the false not only will not recognize the real, but persecute it, just like the church of Jesus' day killed Him. Our Lord is always moving forward with something new and fresh, and it seems in an accelerating fashion. Our focus must continue to be on Him as we walk out each day.

MALACHI FOUR AND THE SPIRIT OF ELIJAH

Malachi was writing about this day that is upon us, that the Spirit of Elijah, The Spirit of the Lord, would be upon us to turn the hearts of the fathers to the children and the hearts of the children to the fathers. This day is the same day that Isaiah wrote about in Chapter 61 prophesying, "The Spirit of the Lord God is upon Me, because the Lord has anointed Me to preach good tidings to the poor; he has sent Me to heal the brokenhearted, to proclaim liberty to the captives, and the opening of the prison to those who are bound; to proclaim the acceptable year of the Lord, and the day of vengeance of our God; to comfort all who mourn in Zion, to give them beauty for ashes, the oil of joy for mourning, the garment of praise for the spirit of heaviness; that they may be called trees of righteousness, the planting of the Lord, that he may be glorified." The Lord Jesus spoke these words when He began His public ministry, in Luke 4:18. He told all in the synagogue that He fulfilled this Scripture in that hour. The Lord is sending forth His Spirit upon those in the earth in the last days who have "cleansed their garments or become trees of righteousness." His Spirit that came upon the Lord and rested upon Him permanently was written about by Isaiah in Chapter 11 verse 1, "There shall come forth a Rod from the stem of Jesse, and a Branch shall grow out of his roots. The Spirit of the Lord shall rest upon Him. The Spirit of wisdom and understanding, the spirit of counsel and might, the spirit of knowledge and of the fear of the Lord." These are the seven spirits of God. We need the reemergence of the apostolic ministry and the return of real fathers that will at first be a harvest of harvesters to usher in the Kingdom of God and expedite His return. Paul wrote that we had many teachers, but not many fathers. Malachi 4 declares this day of the return of the fathers; we will need them.

John writes in Revelation 4, "After these things I looked, and behold, a door standing open in heaven. And the first voice which I heard was like a trumpet speaking with me, saying, 'Come Up here, and I will show you things which must take place after this.'" This Scripture marks a new age which is upon us where the Lord has opened the door (Himself) to heaven and we have open access to Him and His host. Isaiah described a time in Chapter 60 about deep darkness covering the earth, yet he called for us to rise and shine and let our lights shine in this gross darkness. We must "come up here," and know God for our lights to shine. The door standing open in heaven is a demarcation from the Lord standing at the door outside of His church and knocking in Revelation 3, a new era for the body of Christ that brings us into the Kingdom Age, an Age to rule and reign as we tabernacle with King Jesus.

This Kingdom of God is undefinable because Christ is so all encompassing. One way to define this Gospel is the fulfillment of Revelation 11:15 which states, "The kingdoms of this world have become the kingdoms of our Lord and His Christ (us, the anointed ones), and He shall reign forever." He is the KING of Kings and The LORD of Lords. A fully manifested son of God is a Lord and a King, just like the One who has discipled us.

When Adam and Eve first sinned, there was a shift in the power and dominion of the kingdom to darkness from light. We see this when the Lord was taken up to a high place in the wilderness and satan offered to give it back to Him. While the message of the first century church followed the Lord's Gospel of the Kingdom to take back this light, it did not take long for the church to fall away and lose its luster.

The word Kingdom is derived from "King" and "Dominion." We have a mandate from Genesis to be fruitful and multiply, subdue the earth, and walk in dominion, ruling and reigning as kings, sons and daughters. The mountain of the Lord can be thought of as the mountain of all of the combined spheres of influence that make up this larger mountain or kingdom. Celebration, Arts and Entertainment, Education, Government, Economy, etc., are all kingdoms that belong to darkness that we must take back before the Lord's return. Recall in Daniel a small stone became a mighty mountain of the Lord. Daniel saw this kingdom at the end of the age.

In Romans 8, Paul wrote about the Spirit led walk and all of creation groaning and travailing for the manifestation of the sons of God in the Earth. Isaiah wrote about the human child laying down and playing with the cobra, and the lion lying down with the lamb. This is not heaven, but heaven on

Earth as we see in the Lord's Prayer. The Lord has given me a taste of what is to come and made part of the call or purpose of my life to even work in harmony with the animal kingdom to bring order and take dominion in our sphere of influence. Every living and even inanimate object was made to worship and glorify God. Yet the animal Kingdom is most eagerly awaiting the sons and daughters to wake up to their true destinies, not just the animals, but ALL of creation. The water that Jesus walked on longed to be treaded on, and the trees of the forest can't wait to clap their branches, something I have witnessed, when the Lord and His Christ (plural, His anointed ones) manifest on Earth.

JOSEPH, THE ELEVENTH SON TO FORETELL THE ELEVENTH HOUR OF THE CHURCH ON EARTH

I believe that the life of Joseph, a type of Christ, speaks prophetically to the church in the eleventh hour. He was the eleventh son of Jacob. Jacob loved Joseph more than all of his children as he was the son of his old age. He was hated by his brothers; he was sold for twenty pieces of silver. So, Joseph's trials and persecution speak to the wilderness period that God's last days army must go through during preparation for the final hour, represented by Benjamin. We read in Genesis that the Lord was with Joseph mightily, and all that he did prospered. He had favor, even from prison, as long as he was submitted to God and not man. In Genesis 41:41 Pharaoh said that he had set Joseph over all the land of Egypt. This speaks of the dominion and the Gospel of the kingdom that we are called to walk in, just like Joseph. When they suffered through the famine Joseph knew what to do and prepared storehouses. When the money and famine ravished the people of every nation, Joseph was there as a deliverer to save all of Egypt. Egypt speaks of the world and the harvest field. When Joseph "made himself known" to his brothers who thought that he had perished, they were ultimately given the choicest land, the best of the land of Goshen. This speaks of Tabernacles or entering into all of God's promises, crossing the Jordan River, and entering a land flowing with milk and honey and every good thing imaginable. What we see here in the natural foretells what God is doing in spirit or in our hearts and physical bodies. The choice land of Goshen manifests in our bodies so that we are without "spot or wrinkle," literally, but instead life eternal transforms every cell of our bodies, into the likeness of God Himself. Have you ever wondered why some people in the Old Testament lived to be nearly 1000 years old? Don't we have a better covenant? The milk and honey manifests as rivers of living water, in our hearts, flowing to others in the dark world we reside in. And regardless of our circumstances, we are dead to ourselves, deliriously joyful in communion, one with Papa, desiring only to please Him, and serve those around us. Again, all-encompassing and overwhelming, overflowing joy is our strength.

Imagine the Apostle Paul's scripted revelation (1 Corinthian 15:26) that the last enemy to be defeated on planet Earth before Christ's return is literally death itself. Does that include you?

BENJAMIN AND GOD'S LAST DAYS ARMY

During the summer of 2011 Stacey and I invited our mentor Brad to Shreveport for some time of fellowship. Our home group rented a building in the Bossier City River Walk district and spent hours doing evangelism by walking up to complete strangers and asking them if they could recall any dreams that they had had. We interpreted their dreams and then invited them into the building for prophetic ministry and a meeting that evening with Brad. While walking to a nearby restaurant at the conclusion of our meeting for some crazy reason I asked the Lord what tribe Brad belonged to. He spoke very clearly to me, "Benjamin." Later He told me that I too belonged to this same tribe. At the time I had little understanding of what this meant, but have come to grasp the symbology that Jacob's 12 sons were representative of the early, first century church with Reuben, all the way through to Joseph, and the eleventh hour ushering in the last days' church, His tribe of Benjamin. Benjamin, which means "son of my right hand" and speaks to the mighty power of God, was the only son named by His father. This season foretells Tabernacles and refers to the last hour, or the twelfth hour, and those who enter in could be referred to as the tribe of Benjamin, or mature Sons of God, and having become one with Christ, The bride of Christ. When Benjamin sat down to the wonderful meal that Joseph had prepared for Jacob and his sons, he was given five times as much as anybody else. Five is the Lord's number for grace. When Joseph invited Jacob's family to move to Egypt, he gave his brothers a change of clothes, yet he gave Benjamin five changes of clothing and 300 pieces of silver. This speaks to the mighty righteous acts of the last day's Benjamins, walking in His grace, and with supernatural provision. When Jacob knew he was about to die he called together all of his sons and blessed them in order, and to Benjamin he said, "Benjamin is a ravenous wolf, devouring his enemies in the morning and dividing his plunder in the evening." Rachel, Benjamin's mother died in childbirth. We too, God's last days church family, must die to self in order to birth and witness the Benjamins to arise and fulfill this end time's mandate.

PREPARING FOR THE LORD'S RETURN AND THE MILLENNIAL REIGN OF CHRIST ON EARTH

I believe that the Lord allowed me to experience this encounter that I've written about here because He so desperately desires to know me and fellowship with me every day, as His son on this earth. At the time that this happened to me, I was on fire for God, pressing in with all of my might, when suddenly, He revealed Himself to me in ways I would have never dreamed. During the forty-day experience that I had, He permitted me to understand, I believe, the fullness of what it means to be His mature beloved Son on planet earth, and the knowledge and feeling of how much our Dad loves us. He gave me a taste of this so that I could fathom what was coming in the future, and so that I would have the faith to overcome the forthcoming trials in my life, by, very simply but most importantly, first leaning on Him. We are to become love and a habitation for the fullness of His Holy Spirit, once our flesh has become completely sanctified. Sonship and Tabernacles are not about elitism or competition or trying to outrun our brothers and sisters in the Lord — actually, quite the opposite, by helping, serving, and loving the least of the members of our family. The tabernacle of God is made up of outer court believers, inner court believers and those who enter into the fullness of the Melchizedek Priesthood, Kingship, and Lordship with our KING and LORD who went before us. The simplicity of the Gospel is such that we will go as far as our true heart's desire to go with the Lord. It starts with the decisions that we make about being willfully radically obedient to what he wants us to do by serving, yielding to our life, ways, and our own destiny. Or we can choose to do it our way. We can choose life or death, and the freedom he has given us to move up the path of the high calling of God as far as we desire to go.

I am fully persuaded that the most exciting life I could ever live is through following Christ, yet I have found some of the trials I have been in to be so difficult that I have, at times, considered giving up. The path of the mature Christian is not an easy one. It is the memories, the reflections of this encounter and others, and my burning desire to know Him as my Friend, that make me keep going with all of my might. The closer we get to the Lord, the more joy that we have, until potentially one day joy screams and smiles from every cell within our bodies. This life is not about getting born again, and then focusing on what it will be like to be raptured out of here when trouble comes, and then return with the Lord. I am convinced that with every generation, as we read about with the seven churches in Revelation 2,3, that every person that has ever believed God has had an opportunity to be part of the remnant called His Bride, and to partake of the marriage supper of the Lamb. While He will not be returning until He has a bride, a tabernacle of people on the earth walking as He did, without spot or wrinkle, and meeting every need of this world which Papa desires to impact. In the most important sense to me, He has already returned, and desires to tabernacle in and through us. While Jesus is seated on the throne at the right hand of the Father, He is also omnipresent, walking planet Earth, in the midst of those who are desperate for His companionship and the deepest relationship imaginable.

Upon His return, His bride will be a mighty house of faith which operates on the same faith that Jesus did. Just what is this radical faith? When that strong feeling comes over you, deep inside, that gets you completely out of your comfort zone, and doesn't make any sense to family and friends, or logical human reasoning, and that small still voice impresse253s this same exploit upon you; then it is time to exercise radical faith. This is that peace that passes all understanding and requires moving forward into the unknown. Facing the giants that are before us is scary. The radical part is not ever truly having knowledge of the outcome. What we are doing is so often foolish to the natural mind (Romans 8:7), but we must just yield to the Holy Spirit, and believe and trust that Papa will cover our back as we keep going, little by little, towards the Promised Land. Consider all the many examples throughout the entire Bible, the special ones cited in Hebrews 11; they all began as fearful, even at times cowardice in certain areas of their lives. The Lord gave them a task that seemed impossible (or actually was without Him), yet He revealed Himself to them along their Way, and they developed a relationship with their Father, ordinary children of God growing steadily into heroes of this household of faith, radically following what burned inside of them, and only believing that Papa had their backs. Not their will or life's desires, but His. This was and is the most exciting journey imaginable, way beyond what we could possibly come up with, if we only step out of the comfort zone that we live in every day. People like Enoch, Noah, David, Elijah, and you. He has a path, a journey just for you who He so uniquely handcrafted into His very own image and likeness.

Revelation 21: 6, 7 reads, "...I will give of the fountain of the water of life freely to him who thirsts. He who overcomes shall inherit all things, and I will be his God and he shall be My son." This Scripture really summarizes the purpose for the encounter that I am writing about, and why God permitted me to experience this. All that we have to do is run after Him with all of our might, seek Him first to begin every day or situation, and His presence throughout all of our days. Without hesitation, we must be radically obedient as His servant to all that He tells us to do and look for Him in all things and all people. He is our Dad that desires to share all things with us.

JACOB'S LADDER

In Genesis 28 Jacob laid his head on a stone to rest at nightfall and had a dream whereby a ladder came down from heaven to Earth and had angels of God ascending and descending on it. I believe that the rungs of this ladder represent levels of the believer, us, in Christ, with the first rung implying the level of a baby Christian, or newly born-again son of God. With many rungs in between, the highest rung represents God the Creator, or for us, oneness with Father where we flow in the Spirit like our Captain of the host, Jesus. At this level we are more than a bond servant and friend of God, one who walks with Father as close friend, even in an ability to create. The significance of this is that having fully come out of our wilderness experience, we tabernacle with Papa, one with His understanding and wisdom where He no longer needs to feed us mana, but rather we make our own provision, without even thinking about it, by fully trusting in Him for the rest of our days. This is that rest, as He is our Rest that we have so diligently been becoming, to finally enter or climb into.

As I write this, it is 2019, nineteen years after the start of a new millennium. What if the millennial reign of Christ has already begun? What if the second coming of Christ is about Him returning in us first. Wouldn't that really hasten His return? What if all of Paul's writings about the Lords' return were really about when a person dies and stands before the Lord? What if the church's focus on some futuristic event, His return, has gotten us so misguided, that we have missed that He has already returned to walk with us, to rule and reign with us now? What if we can walk and talk with Him on this earth right now just like the twelve did two thousand years ago? How many times have you prayed the Lord's Prayer? Thy Kingdom come, Thy will be done, on earth as it is in heaven? Give us this day our daily bread. Isn't it time that we get still every morning, acknowledge Him all throughout each day, obtain some of this bread of Life so that we know what He wants us to do and be, and taste and run in our true destiny? Isn't it time that we have His answers for a decadent world that is hurting so badly? Wouldn't it be cool if we could be His vessels to serve in meeting the needs of all of the afflicted, or is that really for some future generation?

IN THE NAME OF THE NAME OF THE LORD JESUS CHRIST, WAKE UP!

APPENDIX

SOME OF THE MANY WAYS GOD SPEAKS TO HIS SONS AND DAUGHTERS

I believe that the number of ways the Lord speaks to His kids is infinite, yet I will share a number of ways that He has spoken to me in hopes that you find this section especially edifying. We hear God through His word as He "is and was" the "Word made flesh" according to John. This "word" is essentially three-fold as the inspired written word of God, the Voice that we hear with the eyes of our heart, and the Man, The manifested Word of God, who is walking in the midst of His church. "Word" in the Greek is translated as "*logos*" and also as "*rhema.*" The logos is the informational word of God that we see when we read the Bible, while the rhema word of God is Spirit and Life (Bread) that we hear and see. The Bible states that faith comes by hearing and hearing by the word of God. This "word" is translated *rhema* meaning that we are not operating in faith until we have heard a specific word or words from the Lord so that we can then exercise this faith through that which we have heard. (1)

THE LOGOS WORD OF GOD

God speaks to man through His Holy Scriptures which have been scribed by men, but God-breathed into the Bible. This Book is really a love story from Papa to His sons and daughters; it is a picture of The Bridegroom (Jesus) and His bride (the church). So, every time that we read the Bible we are hearing from God, but this time in study has the potential to be so much more. If we read the Bible to gain knowledge or information, I believe that we will be ever learning but never coming to the knowledge of the truth (2). Ultimately as we read His word beyond its most central meaning, we should be hearing as well, and even having experiences or encounters with Him and His Holy Spirit.

Also important to note are all of the biblical prophecies that we read in the Bible by the Old Testament prophets, many of which have come to pass, yet many others that have not. A couple of examples, and there are hundreds, are as follows. Isaiah wrote sometime near 700 B.C., "For unto us a child is born, Unto us a Son is given; and the government will be upon His shoulder. And His name will be called Wonderful, Counselor, Mighty God, Everlasting Father, Prince of Peace. Of the increase of His government and peace there will be no end, upon the throne of David and over His kingdom, to order it and establish it with judgment and justice from that time forward, even forever. The zeal of The Lord of hosts will perform this." (3) Conceptualize that Isaiah who is often referred to as the messianic prophet, foretold the birth of Christ 700 years before He came. For the point of illustration, the reading of this Scripture for us is time spent in the logos word, yet for Isaiah, he was hearing rhema.

Consider another prophecy, unfulfilled and written by the prophet Daniel. (4) Babylonian King Nebuchadnezzar had a dream that greatly troubled him, so he called all of his sorcerers, astrologers, and magicians, wanting them to first hear his dream from heaven, and then its interpretation. If they could not, he said he would cut them into little pieces and burn their houses down. Daniel prayed, and then had a night vision that revealed both the dream and its interpretation. He saw the huge statue of a man whose head was gold; its chest and arms were silver; the belly and thighs were bronze. It had legs of iron, and feet partly iron and partly clay. A stone which was cut out without hands struck the image, broke everything into pieces and fine dust so that the wind blew all things away, and the stone that struck the image became a great mountain and filled the whole earth. Daniel gave the interpretation that the gold head was King Nebuchadnezzar, with the other parts representing kingdoms that would come after him. He said, "As you saw iron mixed with ceramic clay, they will mingle with the seed of men; but they will not adhere to one another, just as iron does not mix with clay. And in the days of these kings the God of heaven will set up a kingdom which shall never be destroyed; and the kingdom shall not be left to other people; it shall break in pieces and consume all these kingdoms, and it shall stand forever." (5) Many theologians agree that this kingdom is upon us now. We are exiting the Church Age and entering The Kingdom Age which Daniel saw about 2600 years ago.

Imagine a close friend calling you to tell you that he knows what you dreamt last night and also what it means! Now picture yourself doing the same. So, when I read the Bible, I begin with the Logos informational history, story, and testimony that hopefully come alive and bring me into *Rhema*, knowledge, and understanding.

THE RHEMA WORD OF GOD

There are many examples here of the *rhema* word with an emphasis on the unique and different ways that God speaks to His sons and daughters. This catalog of the unimaginatively creative means that our Father speaks to us is infinite. There are many more that I will not be writing about because this list, like Jesus, is without end. It is important to understand that during our lifetimes the Lord actually teaches us how to recognize His voice through our own most special love language that best suits our unique communication with Him. Every time we hear from Him this *rhema* Word transforms us more and ever more from glory to glory, into His image and perfected likeness.

DREAMS

I mentioned previously profound (at least for me) dreams about my spiritual fathers. Sometimes we have simple dreams where the Lord wants to help us. About three years ago we had our house on the market for about three months when my wife Stacey had a dream that gave her the price at which we were meant to have our house listed. Within a few days we had an offer and sold it at the dreamt price. Before you go to bed at night ask Him to give you a dream, and when you have it, don't discount it, but rather get up and scribe it in your journal or a notepad. For me, the first impulse of my mind after I have just dreamt something is to reject that it could have come from God. (6) Generally, upon reflection and help from the Helper, the source of the dream becomes obvious. About eighty-five percent or more of my dreams come from God; some of my dreams that lack color (black and white) reveal the enemies plan for me (called 2nd heaven dreams), or may be from the soul (not my spirit), especially if I've had a long day at work and go to bed mentally wrestling or dwelling on the day's interactions.

In another dream I was speaking to my mother and her mother about a generational character flaw that would leave me if I fasted for ten days. In Job, it reads, "In a dream, in a vision of the night, when deep sleep falls upon men, while slumbering on their beds, then He opens the ears of men, and seals their instruction." (7) I fasted for ten days, eating nothing and drinking only water, and surprisingly had little difficulty being obedient to the instruction of the Lord. The fast started out a little challenging and got easier the longer it went.

VISIONS / NIGHT VISIONS

I also wrote about this earlier. I had a night vision about a cemetery in Venezuela, and in two night visions I had a ticker tape that I could simply read, as the words went across my spirit, while completely awake.

Joel wrote, "And it shall come to pass afterward that I will pour out My Spirit on all flesh; your sons and your daughters shall prophesy, your old men shall dream dreams, your young men shall see visions. And also on My menservants and on My maidservants I will pour out My Spirit in those days." (8) Afterward, I believe refers to the age we are in now; old men dream dreams, and young men see visions. Paul's writing refers to the "old man" as the carnal man or the unsanctified man, so dreams are generally lower level or less important than visions, yet still most helpful and edifying. "Young men" is referring to being like a child to enter the kingdom of God, or having child-like faith (9).

Habakkuk wrote that he would stand his watch to see what the Lord would say to him. Then the Lord answered him and said, "Write the vision and make it plain on tablets, that he may run who reads it. For the vision is yet for an appointed time; but at the end it will speak, and it will not lie.

Though it tarried, wait for it; because it will surely come. It will not tarry." (10)

William Branham, prophet and evangelist, who preached from the mid-1940s until the time of his passing in 1965, had many visions. According to him and others, eyewitness accounts, all of his visions came to pass exactly as the Lord had shown him they would.

OPEN VISION

While I was driving to work about a year ago, I was driving past a long brick wall when I saw a tank blasting holes in the wall. This was most subtle for me, and I initially misinterpreted it. I thought that the Lord was showing me to pray against war that was about to break out somewhere, but He was actually showing me that He was tearing down the hard, brick-like walls of my heart.

OUR SENSES:

SIGHT, SMELL, TOUCH, TASTE, AND HEARING

"O taste and see that The Lord is good; how blessed is the man who takes refuge in Him! (11)

SIGHT OR SEEING

Once I was in a meeting, praying with my eyes closed and I saw, just like in a dream, the rising Sun. Then the rays of the Sun burned a barb wire fence until the wires burned all of the way through. Malachi wrote, "But to you who fear my name -- The Sun of Righteousness shall arise with healing in His wings; and you shall go out and grow fat like stall-fed calves. You shall trample the wicked, for they shall be ashes under your feet on the day that I do this," says the Lord of hosts." (12) With many basic revelations upon hearing from God, we should get the meaning or interpretation, and the application (especially true with dreams). Many times, when we get a revelation like this one, there is also a Scripture that goes with it. (After a dream look at the time on your clock which is often a Scripture.) I have actually had this same revelation several times in meetings. The meaning is that the Spirit of the Lord is providing healing of offenses, for those in the room who are offended at each other (Note the play on words, healing of fences).

God has a tremendous sense of humor and often does this. The seeing gift is especially important to the body of Christ. In the Old Testament we had seers or seer prophets like Samuel. They and we should be able to see kingdom insights with our eyes either open or shut.

SMELL

One morning I was awakened very early to the most powerful, moving, and pleasant floral smell in my bedroom. The aroma of the Lord in our bedroom was waking me up to spend time with Him, and to show me how much He loved me.

TOUCH

When I got filled with the Lord's Holy Spirit, I immediately began to notice that I could feel His presence at a much higher level. When He wants to get my attention about any situation, I generally feel that something is going on. Another example: once I was in a meeting and my eye started to itch. There was nothing wrong with my eye, but several people in the room had eye issues and the healing power of God was there to help. Again, I was in church, and when the guest pastor started speaking, my legs from the shin all of the way to the knee began to burn on both legs. I began to seek the Lord for what He was trying to show me, and it turns out that the speaker had a strong healing gift. Recently during a home meeting, I felt a pressure, like a band around my forehead. The Lord was freeing / renewing or delivering our minds from a worldly / carnal mindset to one more Christ-like.

I recently went through a phase where I kept getting a hot, burning sensation in my right hamstring and buttocks area (biblically the loins). My mentor ultimately helped me understand that these unmistakable feelings were meant to direct me to somebody that needed healing. (13)

TASTE

"Taste and see that The Lord is good." (14) Tasting is much like smelling as we can taste His goodness or tasting bad things in the atmosphere (like metal) can represent demonic activity.

HEARING

Several years ago, I was a High School middle distance running coach at a local private Baptist school. One of the boys I was coaching didn't believe in supernatural healing or that God still spoke to man. Unfortunately, he was partying on his farm and fell out of the back of a moving truck and injured his leg. For about a month we were unable to complete about half of his workouts; he was unable to run hard more than once per week. Then one day while warming up, I distinctly heard the Lord say, "Go tell John that he is healed and can do whatever he wants." My mind went into disbelief and the Lord prompted me again. I pulled the boy aside and told him, confidently. He never missed another practice and went on to finish sixth in the state meet. But more importantly, he experienced God's love firsthand.

There are a number of different types of hearing. We generally hear through the eyes of our hearts, not our audible ears. (15) However, there are some people who have heard the audible voice of God; I have not. The hearing here generally is the soft still voice that we hear as pleasant thoughts that come to our mind when we sit still long enough or wait on the Lord. By waiting I mean quiet meditation. Once, the Lord awakened me in the middle of the night and gave me a Scripture from Colossians that was a message from Him to Stacey, my wife. Another time I had a friend driving me back to work after lunch. As I opened the car door, I very clearly heard, "don't forget your car keys", which were lying on the floor.

Back to my middle-distance coaching; I was at a high school cross country meet near Ruston, Louisiana one Saturday morning. I couldn't help but notice a small Mexican American runner who could run like the wind. As soon as I looked at him the anointing came, and the Lord told me that he would run on an international stage and that his ability and love for Christ would make him a mighty force for the Lord. So, I prayed for about fifteen minutes and sought God as to whether He wanted me to share this with the boy named Enrique. My brain kicked in and made me wonder what his coach might say to me afterwards. Ultimately feeling that I indeed needed to share this with him, I asked the Lord to prepare the way, which he did, and after his race I told him what I heard. He was a believer and immediately knew, by the presence of God, that I had heard from Him, and Enrique was greatly inspired. With this kind of a prophetic word there is the possibility to put pressure on someone where they feel they must try to fulfill the word in their own strength, rather than letting the Lord do the work in His timing. We discussed this and wound up having some terrific conversations about God and running over the next couple of years.

ANGELS

God speaks to his sons and daughters through angels. In the book of Hebrews, we read about ministering angels. By the way, angels may sometimes be saints that have gone on before us. In Revelation 19 John was told by an angel to write or scribe what the angel was telling him. When he fell at his feet to worship him, the angel told him, "See that you do not do that! I am your fellow servant, and of your brethren who have the testimony of Jesus. Worship God! For the testimony of Jesus is the spirit of prophecy." (16) In Daniel we see the archangel Gabriel giving an important message to the prophet. (17) Recall that I have already written about the healing angel that came to me singing, as an answered sign to go pray for the man named Johnny.

IMPRESSIONS

Sometimes we get faint impressions about people or an impression to do something. For me sometimes I just know things about people and sometimes know that I am supposed to do something. Standing in line recently at the grocery store, I got an impression that the elderly lady in front of me had pain in her body. I asked the Lord to give me more, and when we unloaded our groceries, she came walking by me. I knew that I needed to pray for her, and she couldn't wait for prayer once I made the suggestion. Sometimes I may want to do something and contrary to my desire I will get a negative impression like a bad feeling in my head. That is actually the Lord, saying, "not a good idea." Spirit led believers refer to this as being "checked."

FACE TO FACE FROM THE MANIFESTED WORD OF GOD

I long for face to face encounters every day from my Friend and Maker. The Lord spoke to Moses face to face. Biblically, Jesus was seen on seven different occasions after His death for forty days, but before He ascended. I don't think He ever stopped visiting His kids that are hungry for His presence. Matthew wrote, "Blessed are the pure in heart, for they shall see God." (18) We have a promise in John 14:21, that for whomever has and keeps His commandments, He will reveal and manifest Himself to them.

TRANCES

Peter had a trance in the Bible where the Lord told him to kill and eat. (19)

SPIRITUAL GIFTS:

WORD OF KNOWLEDGE, WORD OF WISDOM,
PROPHECY, DISCERNMENT OF SPIRITS,
INTERPRETATION OF TONGUES (20)

WORD OF KNOWLEDGE/
WORD OF WISDOM

After a meeting in Tyler, Texas a young man walked by me and I heard the word "Technology". This was so strong and clear that it was almost like I vomited the word out. It had to come out. I told him that he had a gift for understanding technology. He explained to me that the word was right on.

PROPHECY

A prophetic word is for edification, exhortation, and comfort, and generally has an element of the future in it. That is, it builds up, encourages, and comforts the individual to whom it is given. I was asked by my pastor to pray for one of the praise and worship leaders after church. The Lord directed me to a passage in 1st John in the Bible, and I told him that he was advancing from being a child of God to a young man of the faith. John wrote about little children, young men, and fathers, progressively speaking. (21) This encouraging word was a word of promotion for him, and the Bible passage spoke of young men knowing the word of God and being able to overcome the evil one. All of this was impressed upon me as I shared this with him.

Another time I was sitting on an airplane getting ready for takeoff when a well-known TV sports commentator boarded the plane. When I saw him, the Lord showed me that he was an encourager and that when he came into a room, he had a God given gift that would light everyone up when he began to speak. Scared, I told the Lord that He would have to set this up to confirm that I was supposed to share with him. Sure enough, when I got off of the plane, he walked right up to me and started talking to me. When I gave him the prophecy, he melted and started confessing things to me.

While we are not all prophets, the manifestation gift of prophecy is for ALL believers. "Pursue love, and desire spiritual gifts, but especially that you may prophesy." (22) "For you can all prophesy one by one, that all may learn and all may be encouraged." (23)

INTERPRETATION OF TONGUES

This gift works when a person speaks in tongues and then interprets, or one person may speak in tongues and another interprets. The combination of these two gifts often brings a prophecy, or an understanding of the angelic tongue that was spoken that can now be deciphered in plain English (or another local language) for that person or group. In Jude we read about building ourselves up on our most Holy faith by praying in the Holy Spirit (tongues). Recall that when I visited the former Marine, Johnny, Mike and I heard, "Heal the pain," in plain English while he was praying in the Spirit. (24) When we do this, we will hear from Papa. These last two examples refer to angelic tongues. In Acts 2 we see tongues of men in operation with the 120 from the upper room. They prayed in the Spirit and the multitude of many different nations and languages all heard a message from God in their native tongue or language.

Paul wrote that the greatest gift is love. When we feel compassion towards someone and earnestly desire to help them, Papa generally desires to meet that need through us and His Holy Spirit. This is how Jesus so often functioned in the Bible.

DISCERNMENT OF SPIRITS AND THE GIFT OF UNDERSTANDING

This manifestation gift is given to the body to rightly discern both good and demonic spirits in our atmosphere, generally by simply seeing, feeling, and inquiring about such, so that we know what to pray against. We can't engage in spiritual warfare if we don't know what is warring against us. When we are functioning in love, the Lord will take care of the demonic realm for us and set the captives free. Our focus must always be on the

Lord, and seeing the very best in people like He does, and not by casting our attention on the dark things that we encounter.

Often when the presence of God arrives in our meetings demonic spirits manifest. A friend of mine once complained of a massive headache which represented a pharisaical or religious spirit. Another time I felt intense pressure on the back of my neck, a spirit of death on a gentleman standing in front of me in the kitchen. It is the gift of understanding that intervenes or comes from within to help us grasp what is occurring...a situational awareness or divine understanding.

GOD SPEAKING THROUGH AN INANIMATE OBJECT

One night we had just finished eating and were watching TV when our daughter Sarah's car horn went off in the garage, completely on its own. She was not at home, so I located her spare key and turned off the horn. About five minutes later it happened again, and about five minutes later we were interrupted yet again. I then sought the Lord to learn that He was sounding a trumpet that she was of the age of accountability; He was sounding the battle trumpet / *shofar*, meaning that now was the time that she had become part of His army, and that I really didn't need to help her with anything unless she asked. Sarah had her own walk, and it was time for her to get things on her own.

Years later while entering Chili's restaurant I pushed the clicker to lock my car when another car right in front of me also flashed its lights and beeped the horn. I did this a second time and got the same result. My car and another vehicle which happened to be the same kind and color of the car Sarah drives, beeped, flashed the lights, and locked. This was yet another message that Sarah was entering a new phase of her walk with God, as the green car represented her ride or walk in life.

The green represented a new beginning / growth in her life / walk (vehicle).

GOD SPEAKING THROUGH THE ANIMAL KINGDOM

I have sighted a number of examples here, like the Great Blue Heron I kept seeing, meaning that I was to stand firm in the faith and not be blown around by every wind of doctrine or trying circumstances. The heron often stands patiently still, resting for hours if necessary, to catch its next meal.

In Numbers the Lord opened the mouth of the donkey, and she said to Balaam, "What have I done to you, that you have struck me these three times?"..."Am I not your donkey on which you have ridden all your life to this day? Have I ever been accustomed to do so to you?" Then the Lord opened the eyes of Balaam, and he saw the angel of the Lord standing in the way with drawn sword. (25)

In 2005, I started a small business and knew that I would office downtown, but I had no idea where. So, I parked my car on top of the Chase tower and was looking downtown while seeking God. The anointing came upon me, and my attention was directed to an enormous red-tailed hawk flying over my head. I watched him land on top of the Beck building and immediately knew that was where we were to office. We are still here.

Recently I was driving my truck when I was startled by a Cooper's hawk coming in for a hard landing. He nearly grazed the top of the truck in front of me before aggressively impacting the ground in order to encounter his prey in the hedges to my right. Immediately I heard the word "deliverance," and knew that someone close to me had demonic oppression which needed to be extricated. I then googled the meaning of "Cooper" to learn that a cooper is someone who builds or repairs barrels and vessels. Confirmation!

THROUGH OTHER PEOPLE
(EXAMPLE: WHILE WATCHING A MOVIE)

I was at the movies at year-end a few years ago watching a James Bond movie. At the end of the movie, Bond's boss told James, "It is time to go back to work." Sitting there munching on popcorn when I heard that, the anointing came, and I knew that God was telling me that I was in a new season of hard work. Another time I was watching a TV show called "Burn Notice." The main character was about to engage the enemy and he and two others were extremely outnumbered. The battle was going to begin the next day, and the actor said, "Tomorrow is going to be a long day." When I heard this, I immediately knew that the next year was going to be most trying and difficult. It was, yet the Lord was preparing my heart and mind in advance.

NUMEROLOGY

My wife and I find change often while walking to and from the office, and other places. Some examples: finding a penny can mean that you are a sent one (cent); a nickel may mean grace; a dime may mean order or a call to government; a silver coin can mean that God is doing something redemptive in your life. Sometimes finding change is just that, finding change. It can also mean that He is bringing forth change in ones' life. So, we must be sensitive to His Holy Spirit to determine if He is talking to us.

Most of the time when I stay in a hotel room, especially if I ask the Lord for this, He will give me a Scripture with my room number. Once I stayed in room 167, and when I walked inside there was a Bible opened to the following passage from Psalm 16:7, "I will bless the Lord who has given me counsel; my heart also instructs me in the night seasons." While I was there, I had dreams from the Lord which gave me instruction. Another time a friend of mine was staying in room 220. Immediately I knew that his room number was a message from the Lord about Galatians 2:20 being a destiny Scripture for him. Another time I was visiting a friend who was staying in room 534. He was going through a difficult trial and when I heard his room number I knew that it was a message for him from Isaiah 53:4 that, "Surely He (the Lord) has borne our griefs and carried our sorrows"... meaning that my friend needed to let go of this grief and sorrow, and give it back to Jesus who had already taken this upon Himself at the cross.

Stacey and I were riding our bikes one day in a rural area when we heard a jingling noise. We looked down and saw coins. We got off of our bikes and picked up 386 coins and three one-dollar bills. I am not exaggerating; this was crazy, like a treasure hunt, finding coins in the grass on both sides of the road. Stacey got upset with me because I spent some of the change in parking meters, and she wanted to put the coins in a jar for a keepsake. (She should have told me, ha!) We couldn't put them all in our pockets, so we finished our twenty something mile ride, and then returned in the car to pick up the rest. We believe that this message was about evangelism. As we found many different types of coins from several countries and many denominations of coinage, we felt this spoke of the evangelical outreach to many denominations and ethnic groups. We started on our bikes but wound up in our car. Vehicles speak of ministry or our walk. In this case we grew from bicycles to a Suburban SUV family vehicle.

Once a Jewish attorney handed me his business card and when I looked at the address, 333 Texas Street, the anointing came, and I heard Jeremiah 33.3. To this day I have still not revealed this to him, asking the Lord for the right timing. He may just have to read the book! Jeremiah 33:3, "Call to me, and I will answer you and show you great and mighty things, which you do not know." The Lord really wants to reveal Himself to this man in spectacular fashion.

THROUGH A PARABOLIC NATURAL OCCURRENCE

By parabolic, I mean, like a parable. I just gave an example above, finding change in the country. In 1998 when I was lost (not yet born again) and still belonged to satan and the dark side, I was in a bicycle race that went up a mountain in Arkansas called Rich Mountain. The race was twelve miles uphill with 2000 feet of climbing. I won the race in 41 minutes and 41 seconds, with a winning margin of five seconds. Years later I was driving up the mountain and shared this story with my friend Mickey. He looked at me when I told him my time and said, "That's a Scripture." The Holy Spirit immediately gave witness to his statement.

I went home later and prayed and realized that this was Genesis 41:41 (the only 41:41 in the Bible) and the bike race was a message from God, yet amazingly this parable came at a time when I was still lost and living in the world, spiritually. (Think John 3:16.) The race spoke of a destiny message for me that I was to work on God's mountain of riches or economy as a businessman. Five is His number for grace, the winning margin. The Scripture from Genesis was about taking dominion in my sphere of influence, finance. The 2000 feet of climbing spoke of Gods' dominion returning to the earth in His sons and daughters 2000 years after Christ. In the race I beat two people on the US national team. They were arguing with a race official afterwards that there was no way that I could have won. This also spoke of God using a "regular, normal guy" like me to confound the wise and beat the so-called professionals.

THE LORD OFTEN SPEAKS TO US THROUGH OUR WALK AS A PROPHETIC PARABLE

Our lives are often a prophetic parable. I recall hearing the phrase "first in the natural, then the spiritual." A few of many examples in my life follow. During my elite running days, I never met anybody (no exaggeration) that could outrun me downhill. This natural gift spoke to my walk as a son of God. I am diligently laboring to enter His rest which is like effortless downhill running. Similarly, when I was more than a few pounds lighter, I had a great natural ability to climb mountains on a bicycle (see last paragraph). This clearly speaks spiritually of a time in the future to climb to the top of Mount Zion, or the mountain of the Lord. My gift as an endurance athlete speaks to my ability to endure things, as it is through much tribulation that we enter the kingdom of God. Before I was even born again, I always had a sense in potentially dangerous situations (think military flying) that I would survive, like the God of eternity was looking out for me....that I would survive and thrive in any radical situation that I was confronted with. This spoke to me, imprinted upon me, burned within me, as if marked or called out by Papa ... that His hand was on my life, that I was a long-term survivor, a creature of eternity.

THIS BOOK

A central theme to this book goes with the first sentence which was also a manifestation of the first miracle in my life (Remember Mike and I praying for the man in the coma.) "In the name of the Lord Jesus Christ, wake up." I believe that the Lord was trying to wake me up to who I am in Him! Once that has become a reality for me, I can then help others to wake up to who they are in Christ Jesus.

THE LORD SINGING

During November of 2009 I woke up one morning with the Lord singing to me. He was singing to me that there was no one like me. I felt like I was in the clouds all day, feeling incredibly special, even unique among the unique, that He had meticulously handcrafted me into something He felt was great. He desperately wanted me to know and feel that, and His unwavering love for me.

SUPERNATURAL EXPERIENCES

The next two messages from the Lord were nothing short of breathtaking for me, yet I did need some help from my mentor for the meaning.

SEALED FOR SERVICE

I was at a prophetic conference in Shreveport a few years ago listening to a speaker named Chuck Pierce. In the middle of his message I noticed that my left elbow was getting warm, then all of the sudden it was burning hot, and a blister immediately bubbled up on my forearm near my elbow. A few days later a scab formed and when the scab fell off, I had a brand on my arm in the shape of a fish. You cannot imagine the love I felt from Papa that He would do this to me. "Now He who establishes us with you in Christ and has anointed us is God, who also has SEALED us and"... God was telling me that at this juncture in time He sealed me for His service. (26)

GIANT ORB

I don't recall exactly when this happened, I think just a couple of years after our encounter. Stacey and I were on a plane flying to Cincinnati and connecting to somewhere else on the east coast. I recall asking the Lord to speak to us while awaiting takeoff. Once we climbed to our cruising altitude, I looked out the left window and saw an enormous Orb like the Sun, but much larger. It stayed there, I think until our descent started. I recall a young boy (childlike faith) getting really excited and shouting at it and getting the stewardess, but no one else seemed to even notice it, like it was some kind of reflection off of the plane or something. This was Papa and He was saying to us, "I will never leave you nor forsake you." How cool is that? We love Him because he first loved us.

PUTTING MANY OF THESE TOGETHER

While I have listed all of these ways that Papa speaks to His kids separately, hearing from Him often means combining several of these ways in one setting. For example, sometimes in spiritual meetings, my palms will get oily. This always means that God's healing touch is there to heal whoever needs it. So, when that happens, the next step automatically for me is to start asking for Him to show me who has something wrong and what it is. He might speak next, or perhaps my left knee would start to hurt (if someone has a left knee issue). Or perhaps I close my eyes, and He gives me a picture of something. You get the sense of how creative our God is. He speaks very differently to each one us as well, in the love language that He has for each one of us, individually.

CULTIVATING HIS GIFTS, SEEING, AND HEARING HIS VOICE

While the gifts and callings of God are without repentance, (27) it is most important that we and our children go through Pentecost and get baptized by Jesus so that we can really engage the revelatory realm and know Papa so much more each day. I can recall after my Pentecostal experience that I went to a prophetic conference in Texarkana, Arkansas with my friends Mickey and Jack. Jack's son, Brad, was the speaker for the conference. We made the hour and a half drive for a morning of teaching that was followed by spiritual exercises to practice seeing into the revelatory realm and hearing God's voice. They would put a person on a chair at the front and then give everyone a minute or two to get whatever God was speaking to that person. This was the first time that I ever encountered anything like this, and I can recall that that day I did not hear or see anything. While I believe that the Lord takes us through dry seasons, this was not the case for me;

I had just never really been exposed to this before, and I was not very sensitive to the Holy Spirit; I found myself trying too hard, not resting in Him. I write this to share that I don't consider myself to be terribly spiritual; it took me a few months of sincere practice to hear and see from God seemingly sporadically. With each revelation there is so much excitement, and I still feel today like a little kid, really just getting started with knowing Jesus.

Initially I found my spiritual awareness to be embarrassing, yet I was shown a framework for me and my family to practice hearing from God, something and Someone to really go after. We must fear God and not man by not caring what people think when we get things wrong. This is so important for church settings to foster the development of the gifts, and to understand that we all miss it sometimes. Missing God does not make you a false prophet if you are genuinely sincere. It is character flaws that identify false prophets. Jesus said that you shall know them by their fruit. (28) The Lord also put a hunger in me to hear and see and to know Him, so I went to a lot of prophetic conferences. My recollection is that for a few months it seemed like God did not want to talk to me in these settings. However, as time progressed, I learned that He wants to speak with me far more than I desire to hear from Him. I just needed to exercise my spiritual senses and get in tune with what the Spirit was saying. This is a lifelong process.

I believe that the main purpose for belonging to a church fellowship is to worship Him, but also to grow in the Lord to maturity, so that we can ultimately be sent out to the world and know what to do or say in every situation; we are called to have or be the answer. A study of Ephesians 4 talks about God's government and the equipping of the saints for service. We should all hope to grow into leadership roles to help others in the church and our families. This requires that we are connected to the people whom God has chosen to align us.

My wife and I, for a season, would get our four girls together in the living room and do spiritual exercises to show them that they could hear from God. I can't wait to do this with my grandchildren. It was amazing how He revealed Himself unto us during this season. We also went to a local school at Christian Center of Shreveport that they had in the fall to teach people the prophetic ministry. We would meet once a week for a teaching and then do exercises. This would include going out into the field every other week and practicing dream interpretation and prophesying over people at the local mall. It is amazing what you can learn by going out with a friend and doing this, and how God is always faithful and meets us in our exploits, regardless of our maturity level. More importantly, it is incredible to see people get touched when you tell them what their dream means, and that they too hear from heaven, or you tell them something that they know only could have come from the Father (prophecy), that is edifying, exhorting, and comforting to them.

END NOTES

PART I

1. Mark 16:18, James 5:14-15, Hebrews 6:2
2. Romans 10:17
3. Mark 11:23
4. John 6:44
5. John 3:3, John 3:16-17
6. John 14:26
7. Colossians 2:9, "For in Him (Christ) dwells all the fullness of the Godhead bodily."
8. Acts 4:12, note that this Scripture is from Peter, a Jew, "Nor is there salvation in any other for there is no other name (Jesus) under heaven given any man by which we must be saved."
9. 2 Timothy 3:16,17, "All Scripture is given by inspiration of God, and is profitable for doctrine, for reproof, for correction, for instruction in righteousness, that the man of God may be complete, thoroughly equipped for every good work."
10. John, Chapter 1
11. Hebrews 13:8
12. Colossians 1:9-12
13. Ephesians 1:15-23
14. 1 Corinthians 4:20
15. 1 Corinthians 14:1
16. Acts 4:33
17. Matthew 3:11

18. Hebrews 5:14, understanding through experience.
19. Mark 16:15-20
20. Ephesians 2:8,9
21. 1 Corinthians 12:7-11
22. 1 Corinthians 12:9
23. Matthew, Chapter 10
24. Matthew 10:8
25. 1 Corinthians, Chapter 12
26. Acts 19:6
27. Acts 2:4, 1 Corinthians 14:15
28. In Mark 6:2-6 we read that Jesus could not do many miracles in Nazareth except to place His hands on a few sick people and heal them. This was due to their unbelief or lack of faith. We must balance this with a truth that certainly God can do or use man to do whatever He wills. Understand also that Jesus had no special privileges (use of His divinity) when He walked the Earth (Philippians 2:5-8), and He was only interested in seeking, discovering, and doing the will of His Father. (John 5:19,20)
29. Hebrews 13:8
30. Mark 9:28,29
31. Matthew 7:6
32. 2 Peter 3:9
33. 2 Corinthians 4:3,4

Part II

34. Hebrews 4:12
35. Acts 1:5, Acts 2:38, 1 Corinthians 14:26
36. Mark 16:16, Acts 8:16
37. Hebrews 13:8
38. Ephesians 4:11-16
39. Ephesians 4:11
40. Judges 1:6,7
41. I have read and studied a new revelation about the progression of the believer from being born again, to disciple, servant, friend, and finally, son of God. According to Rick Joyner of Morningstar ministries the first century church well understood the relevance of the progression so that one could easily determine where he / she was and then move on to the next level. We must also contrast this understanding by being focused on the Lord and not on ourselves. Still, the hand becomes most helpful, again, in explaining the maturation process of most believers. The small finger represents the born again believer who, generally, by sound teaching and an understanding through faith in the finished work of the cross by our Savior, comes to the Lord; the ring finger represents the disciple, so through pastoring and shepherding one becomes a disciple and begins to disciple his own converts; the evangelical, longest reaching middle finger represents the servant, think missions or outreach; the index

finger representative of a friend of God has grown to really know Papa, so much so that he is entrusted with deep secrets like the prophet of God; and finally the thumb represents the sons of God. Again, the thumb can touch all other fingers meaning that the believer functions in all five, and the thumb is so foundational to God's government on the earth. All of creation is groaning and travailing for the manifestation of the sons of God (most loving / mature believers) in the earth (Romans 8). There are a number of Scriptural references for articulating this progression of the believer, but most notable is John, Chapter 15.

42. 1 Corinthians 14:26

43. Revelation 2

44. John 10:10

45. John 14:21, Jesus will reveal or manifest Himself to you.

46. Zechariah 4:7

47. 1 Corinthians 12:8, A word of knowledge is a word / revelation that is heard from God, spoken from one person and directed to another. The receiver of God's word generally should have a helpful accompanying interpretation and application.

48. Ephesians 4:11, Recall the hand, fingers, and thumb.

49. Ephesians 4

50. Matthew 16:25

51. Revelation 2:1-7

52. Numbers 12:6

53. Numbers 11:29

54. Ephesians 5:27

55. 1 Corinthians 15:6

56. Revelation 13:8

57. John 8:56

58. Romans 8:34, Ephesians 1:20

59. Hebrews 13:8

60. Hebrews 12:1

61. Genesis 28:11-19

62. Hebrews 13:2

63. John 14:21

64. Luke 24

65. Luke 24:32

66. Matthew 25:34-40

67. Romans 8:18-25

68. Ephesians 5:27

Part III

69. Romans 12:6-8, redemptive gifts

70. Leviticus 23, mandatory in the Old Testament, celebratory for spiritual Israel

71. Colossians 1:15, Romans 8:29

72. John 11:25

73. Revelation 3,4

74. Acts 11:26, 26:28

75. Ephesians 2, Romans 11

76. Exodus 12

77. Philippians 2:5-8

78. Matthew 12:40

79. In Acts 8:12-14 we see people of Samaria becoming born again and getting water baptized after their conversions, having heard the word of God from Philip. Following, in verse 15, we see Peter and John traveling from Jerusalem to Samaria to pray for them to receive "the Holy Spirit." Clearly, this represents a higher level (They were already born again.) with God, a baptism from Jesus that John the Baptist wrote about, entering us into Pentecost. Another like example is found in Acts 19:2 where Paul asks Apollos and others if they have received the Holy Spirit since they became believers. Apollos had previously been referred to as "mighty in the Scriptures", and "fervent in Spirit, he spoke and taught accurately the things of the Lord, though he knew only the baptism of John." In Acts 19:6 Paul laid hands on him and others; they received the baptism of the Holy Spirit, Pentecost, and immediately spoke in tongues and prophesied.

80. John 14:21

81. Galatians 2:20

82. Zechariah 14:16-21

Appendix Notes

1. Romans 10:17
2. 2 Timothy 3:7
3. Isaiah 9:6,7
4. Daniel 2
5. Daniel 2
6. Romans 8:7
7. Job 33:15
8. Joel 2:28,29
9. Matthew 18:3
10. Habakkuk 2
11. Psalm 34:8
12. Malachi 4:2,3
13. Discernment, 1 Corinthians 12:10
14. Psalm 34:8
15. Ephesians 1, Psalm 34:8
16. Revelation 19:10, Hebrews 1:14
17. Daniel 8:16, 9:21
18. Matthew 5:8
19. Acts 10
20. 1 Corinthians 12
21. 1 John 2:12-14
22. 1 Corinthians 14:1
23. 1 Corinthians 14:31
24. Jude 20
25. Numbers 22
26. 2 Corinthians 1:21,22
27. Romans 11:29
28. Matthew 7:20